19082534

The Rhetoric
of Dreams

Bert O. States

Cornell
University
Press   Ithaca and London

First published 1988 by Cornell University Press.

International Standard Book Number 0-8014-2198-5
Library of Congress Catalog Card Number 88-47766
Printed in the United States of America
*Librarians: Library of Congress cataloging information
appears on the last page of the book.*

*The paper in this book is acid-free and meets the guidelines for permanence
and durability of the Committee on Production Guidelines for Book
Longevity of the Council on Library Resources.*

For Dan McCall

Contents

Acknowledgments

P ARTS OF this book appeared first in essay form as the following: "The Art of Dreaming," *Hudson Review* 31 (Winter 1978–79): 571–586; "I Think, Therefore I Dream," *Hudson Review* 39 (Spring 1986): 53–80; "Dream and Memory," *Dreamworks* 3 (1983): 153–159. I thank the editors of the *Hudson Review* and *Dreamworks* for permission to use those essays in greatly revised form. I owe a special debt to Frederick Morgan and his editors at *Hudson* for their long-standing encouragement in this and other projects of mine. I also want to acknowledge the careful and, as usual, inspiring reading of the manuscript by my friend and colleague Paul Hernadi of the University of California at Santa Barbara.

B.O.S.

Santa Barbara, California

The Rhetoric of Dreams

People who dream when they sleep at night . . . know that the real glory of dreams lies in their atmosphere of unlimited freedom. It is not the freedom of the dictator, who enforces his own will on the world, but the freedom of the artist, who has no will, who is free of will. The pleasure of the true dreamer does not lie in the substance of the dream, but in this: that there things happen without any interference from his side, and altogether outside his control. Great landscapes create themselves, long splendid views, rich and delicate colours, roads, houses, which he has never seen or heard of. Strangers appear and are friends or enemies, although the person who dreams has never done anything about them.

—Isak Dinesen, *Out of Africa*

The dreams were eloquent, but they were also beautiful. That aspect seems to have escaped Freud in his theory of dreams. Dreaming is not merely an act of communication (or coded communication, if you like); it is also an aesthetic activity, a game of the imagination, a game that is a value in itself. Our dreams prove that to imagine—to dream about things that have not happened—is among mankind's deepest needs.

—Milan Kundera, *The Unbearable Lightness of Being*

Introduction

I N AN EFFORT to explain the transformation of matter that might take place in the "black hole" in deep space, the physicist S. Chandrasekhar tells an old Indian parable about the dragonfly at the bottom of a pond:

> A constant source of mystery for these larvae was what happens to them when, on reaching the stage of chrysalis, they pass through the surface of the pond, never to return. (Each larva, as it feels impelled to rise to the surface and depart) promises to return and tell those that remain behind what really happens, and to confirm or deny a rumor attributed to a frog that when a larva emerges on the other side of their world it becomes a marvelous creature with a long slender body and iridescent wings. But on emerging from the surface of the pond as a fully formed dragonfly, it is unable to penetrate the surface no matter how much it tries and how long it hovers. (As with someone who might fall into a black hole, communication is irrevocably cut off.)[1]

[1] As reported by Walter Sullivan in an interview with S. Chandrasekhar. See Walter Sullivan, "Curiouser and Curiouser: A Hole in the Sky," *New York Times Magazine*, July 14, 1974, p. 35. The words in parentheses are Sullivan's paraphrase of Chandrasekhar.

The parable illustrates the plight of the dreamer who awakens and hovers on the surface of consciousness, freshly exiled from the deep world of the dream he has just left behind. Fortunately, unlike the dragonfly, he may return to another sector of this world in another dream. But again, on waking, he will enact the loss of that *place* in which he suspects lie the secrets of his being, or at least a part of his being that seems to go on without him. Even the terrifying dream holds its nostalgia for the dreamer, for it is as real, in the phenomenal sense, as his waking life. Some, like Antonin Artaud, would argue that the dream is even more real, in the sense that it intensifies experience that is normally diluted by daily life.

Of course, the dreamer will tell his dream to a friend not to communicate its story but to prevent a complete loss of the experience. There is always that overwhelming fact that he is the only *real* person who was *there,* and this is a disturbing form of loneliness (how can this experience be allowed to pass into oblivion without witness?). But the telling is not the dream. So there he is, a dragonfly again—first in his waking, then in his telling others what he has awakened from.

As a model, the parable of the dragonfly will not tell us much about dreaming, but it does express our common frustration in leaving behind a vein of experience that seems to divide our life cycle into two primary states of consciousness. Probably most people would say, "Dreaming is dreaming. Why worry about it?" And some readers of this book will surely ask, "How is it that I can live—be fully conscious in—two such different worlds?" Finally, there are those who have a professional interest in dreams, of whom there are three main varieties. The most familiar school of thought is the psychological-psychoanalytic, which is substantially experimental and diagnostic: When and how long do we dream? What are the signals of dreaming? What is the function of dreaming? And what do dreams tell us about the dreamer? The second and newest school is the neurophysiological, which is concerned principally with brain activity, of which the dream is a unique phenomenon bearing on the nature of memory and the storage of information. The third is the philosophical school, which is largely worried about the epistemological validity of the dreaming experience: Do we dream? Are dreams experiences? Why do we forget dreams?

While these schools of thought overlap somewhat in their approaches to dreams, they represent three different concepts of dreaming that are supported by three different kinds of data. Psychoanalysts (and many psychologists) think of dreaming as a mode of neurosis transportation and are therefore interested in the "load" dreams bear; neurophysiologists look only at the vehicle bearing the load; philosophers are not really sure there is a load or a vehicle to bear one, because nothing can be taken as granted in philosophy until it has been submitted to the rigor of thought. If you put the most tolerant representative of each school adrift in the same boat for a very long time, a unified theory of dreaming might emerge, but you would probably have more luck getting agreement about God from the Catholic, the Protestant, and the Jew in one of those old jokes.

My own approach to the dream is in some respects a compound of these three schools in that I make use of the findings of psychologists, philosophers, ·scientists, and where possible, phenomenologists (who are among the most intrepid of philosophers) like Merleau-Ponty, Sartre, and Bachelard. But in a more basic sense my approach is what I can broadly call humanistic. It is concerned with the possible relationship of dreaming to all imaginative activity and thought—primarily art. But even more particularly, I am interested in the dream as an experience that is both private and universal, and my main concern is to say what can be said about the experience itself—hence the phenomenological bias. What are the characteristics of the dream? What is left behind when we enter the dream state? What is amplified in the dream state? How are dreams organized? How do they resemble, and differ from, the imaginary fictions of the artist? the productions of language? In short, I take it for granted that dreams are experiences because I have them. If a philosopher should prove to me on solid logical grounds that dreams are not experiences, or that we only think we dream, or dream we dream, and that therefore the thing we refer to as a dream is a delusion, I would still want to write about dreams as I do. If it was a delusion that woke me last night in a cold sweat, it was a convincing one, and I can depend on being deluded again tonight. We are such stuff as these delusions are made of.

Thanks mainly to Freud, the dream has been overwhelmingly in the hands of the psychologists. We cannot blame the psychologists for this, because they have proper business with the dream. But few humanist scholars have bothered to look directly at the dream as a subjective experience that has, however delusively, aroused in us all a sense of being alive in an unusual way. One scholar will write about Kafka and the dream, another about Mann or Strindberg and the dream, but few write about the dream itself. The average person is so used to dreaming that dreaming becomes as unremarkable as shaving or daydreaming on the bus. Yet for several hours each night, most of us invent and populate an outrageous world into which we are involuntarily projected, to take our chances like the hero of a novel or a film. This is a staggering fact about human consciousness, this *other* reality—if you define reality as whatever you think you are in. Consequently, there is this dragonfly need to slip back inside the dream, with all your waking faculties intact, to spy on it,

4

force its secret, and then get back out with the treasure, like the great white hunter. Unfortunately, however, you must leave all these things at the door, and once inside you are one of the native flatlanders.

This frustration introduces the question of whether it is legitimate to use the remembered distortions of dreams as evidence of anything substantial. Can a recalled dream be used as a "text" in the sense that we use literary texts as a ground of theory about such texts? My conclusion is that the reliability of my dreams, or the dreams of others that I quote, depends not on the accuracy of the dream-report but on its resemblance to dreams my reader may have had. Ideally, there will be a metaphorical realization that dreams are "like this" or that "I have dreamed of that myself." The evidence is evocative at best, far from scientific. Early on, it occurred to me that anyone who writes about dreams finds himself in the situation of the medieval cartographers who mapped the Atlantic Ocean with places and creatures born of tales told by others or of their own imaginations. This is the problem with all dream theory from Freud forward, and a phenomenological study of dreams can scarcely hope to escape it. But then, this is the difficulty with all speculation about what goes on in the mind. There is no empirical science of mind, and as Daniel Dennett puts it, we are reduced to an "aprioristic reasoning about *what must be*—what thoughts must be, what meaning must be, what symbols must be, and so forth."[2] We can only proceed with a mixture of self-observation and a little method derived from the tradition of scientific guesswork.

Primarily, my book is a rhetoric of dreams (Part Two). To my knowledge, Emile Benveniste is the first person to

[2]Daniel C. Dennett, "Why We Think What We Do about Why We Think What We Do: Discussion on Goodman's 'On Thoughts without Words,'" *Cognition* 12 (1982): 219.

suggest, within a Freudian context, that one might write a rhetoric of oneiric language using "the old catalogue of tropes."[3] But so far as I know, the present book is the first sustained look at the dream and dreaming from a tropological perspective. My conception of the figurations of dreams, however, is radically different from the one projected by Benveniste. Two of my central assumptions are that the dream is not a repressive mechanism and that it is not a form of language. Both these assumptions diverge from modern linguistic and psychoanalytic theory, particularly as these converge in the French Freudians, who have long since implanted metaphor and metonymy in the unconscious. What I maintain—if I may reverse Jean-François Lyotard's notion—is that the dream does not speak, it thinks.[4] It manifests strategies of thought that if traced upward into language would eventuate in the master tropes. So dreams are a kind of proto-rhetoric, *not yet* a language. Hence, one way to study them might be to see how the principles of rhetoric—the four master tropes, in this case—could be traced *back into* the dream-work, bearing in mind that in applying verbal structures to preverbal structures we are already speaking an odd sort of metaphor. All in all, I might sum up my perspective as a phenomenological rhetoric of dreaming.

One or two points of orientation are in order before I proceed to my argument. A rhetorician might complain that I have extended the definitions of the tropes beyond any form of recognition or taxonomic usefulness. My case will have to rest on my individual discussions in Part Two. What I am trying to see, through the tropes, is how our

[3]Emile Benveniste, *Problems in General Linguistics,* trans. Mary Elizabeth Meek (Coral Gables, Fla.: University of Miami Press, 1971), p. 75.

[4]Jean-François Lyotard, "The Dream-Work Does Not Think" (trans. Mary Lydon), *Oxford Literary Review* 6 (1983): 3–34.

most involuntary form of visual thinking might be articulated in their transactions. The problem in writing about the dream is that there is no ready language for converting its mechanism into descriptive discourse. There is the language of psychoanalysis, it is true, and the psychoanalyst might complain that I have simply given Freud's principles other names: metonymy and synecdoche = condensation; metaphor = displacement; irony = contradiction, and so on. To that I can only say that Freud's processes, as processes, are perfectly good—in fact, unavoidable—though I had worked on dreams for many years before it occurred to me that there were strong parallels between the master tropes and Freud's dream processes. I take these parallels as an indication that in using them, in either their Freudian or tropological forms, we are coming about as close to the origins of dream formation as we are likely to get, and it is suggestive that one of our more vigorous projects remains the translation of Freud's theory into tropological terms. In my own case, it was neither Freud nor rhetoric that primarily interested me, but the dream-work itself, and to have used Freud's principles of dream formation would have been confusing and quixotic, given my differences with psychoanalytic assumptions about the ends served by the principles.

So for my project the master tropes offered the clearest and most elementary conceptual vocabulary available to a phenomenological understanding of the dream process. To the classical rhetorician who believes that the tropes were not intended for this use, I would point out that we are steadily writing books and essays and holding conferences on metaphor, metonymy, and irony (synecdoche has had a more modest press and usually gets into such discussions on the coattails of metonymy). Surely the reason must be that, despite our ongoing debate about how much domain to allow each trope, we are beginning to see that tropes involve "primitive" and "undecomposable" strategies of thought, in the words of George Lakoff and Mark Johnson.[5] Physicists speak of fundamental transactions at the "bottom" of the material world—gravity, electromagnetism, the weak force, and the strong force. I do not want to draw suggestive analogies between matter and mentation, but with the tropes we are working at *that level* of description. And I note in passing that the physicist regularly has recourse to metaphors in order to arrive at descriptions of the forces that drive the real world. Chandrasekhar's conception of the black hole (already a metaphor) as a pond in which matter is irrevocably transmogrified will not bring about useful advances in cosmology, but it does get the phenomenon out of interstellar gas and into some form of model, if only one that pacifies our interim ignorance about something so stupendous as a light-consuming ball hanging in distant space.

This leads to the question "At what point does neuronal activity become "psychological"? At what point does chemistry turn into behavior? However mythical, such a point would seem to be the organic equivalent of a black hole in outer space in that it is the site of a translation of matter into memory, or memory into matter. Thus, we might take Foucault's metaphor almost literally—imagination exists "at the suture of body and soul."[6] Such a metaphor reminds us that thought has a chemical foundation and that we have no frog, or amphibian, who knows both sides of the pond's surface. The neuroscientists are working virtually *at* the site with excellent measuring instruments, but as humans themselves they are using metaphors left and right ("gating," "mapping," "wiring,"

[5]George Lakoff and Mark Johnson, *Metaphors We Live By* (Chicago: University of Chicago Press, 1980), p. 72.

[6]Michel Foucault, *The Order of Things: An Archaeology of the Human Sciences* (New York: Vintage, 1973), p. 70.

"zone mailing," "tuning") to convert their machines' readings into findings. You may think that these metaphors are simply explanatory devices for the lay audience, so much icing on the cake, and that for the scientist only hard facts give rise to conclusions. But conclusions, particularly in new sciences, are often long in coming and in the interim are likely to take the form of metaphorical constructions that project suspected features of a phenomenon in an analogical form. These are called "theory-constitutive metaphors," and as Richard Boyd says, they are useful chiefly because "they provide a way to introduce terminology for features of the world whose existence seems probable, but many of whose fundamental properties have yet to be discovered."[7] In other words, a theory-constitutive metaphor, as opposed to a pedagogical metaphor, is one that indicates "a research direction" (p. 407). In thinking aprioristically, or metaphorically, about the brain, then, one might say that in order to produce *this* capability (say, the power of association), there must be a structure in the brain that resembles a system of maps, and that with this map in hand one might then go looking in the neuronal countryside for whatever it is that is *like* a map that makes associative thought possible. So metaphors, as we know them, are only the tip of metaphorical thinking.

Meanwhile, at the other end of the hall the psychoanalysts, clinical and literary, are relying even more heavily on metaphors to describe certain products—traumas or texts—of the same chemical processes. If you read any amount of the literature from both ends of the hall, you

[7]Richard Boyd, "Metaphor and Theory Change: What Is 'Metaphor' a Metaphor For?" in *Metaphor and Thought*, ed. Andrew Ortony (Cambridge: Cambridge University Press, 1986), p. 364. See also the reactions to Boyd's essay by Thomas S. Kuhn and Zenon W. Pylyshyn in the same collection.

will soon realize how long the hall actually is, yet at the same time how contiguous the two enterprises at either end are. The neuroscientists have little curiosity, and some skepticism, about a concept like the unconscious—at least, as Jean-Pierre Changeux says, it teaches them very little about the functions and mechanisms that produce mental images.[8] And, with notable exceptions, psychoanalysts have little interest in the discoveries of neuroscience.[9] This is neither surprising nor unusual, because what psychoanalysts do with the unconscious for their own purposes probably has little to do with the physiology of the brain. As Jim Swan has put it, "quantified and objective scientific concepts are necessarily incapable of describing one's *experience* of one's own body."[10] In any case, in the present work I submit the unconscious and its companion principles of repression and censorship to my own critique, primarily because I believe we need an alternative to the psychoanalytic study of dreams and dream functions. So deeply ingrained in our thought is the idea of the unconscious that if someone could definitively prove that the unconscious does not exist, or that it exists only in the form of "deep" associative thinking (as I maintain here), it would have little effect on our continuing study of "its" behavior and influence. The unconscious has become that part of our mystery in which we can plant the flag of intellectual conquest even as we claim that it cannot be understood. Even the deconstructivist enterprise, whose

[8]Jean-Pierre Changeux, *Neuronal Man: The Biology of Mind*, trans. Laurence Garey (New York: Pantheon, 1985), p. 152.

[9]One of the most accessible books, not only for its application of neuroscience to psychoanalysis, but also for its clear explication of the psychoanalytic process itself, is Morton F. Reiser, *Mind, Brain, Body: Toward a Convergence of Psychoanalysis and Neurobiology* (New York: Basic Books, 1984).

[10]Jim Swan, "*Mater* and Nannie: Freud's Two Mothers and the Discovery of the Oedipus Complex," *American Imago* 31 (Spring 1974): 56.

origins are as much in psychoanalysis as in linguistics, is one that would put the *formulation* of deferral, as an act of the investigative ego, in the nonplace of deferral itself. And if Freud has done nothing else, he has given a habitation, a name, and a few operational principles to this place in us that is *never here,* a place that, as it turns out, has offered us another systematic way of doing everything all over again. To locate the repressed, or the still deconstructable, is today the paramount preoccupation of our commentary.

My quarrel is not with the discipline of psychoanalysis, but rather with the concept of the unconscious, refined mainly through the study of dreams, that has made the dream little more than a highway leading to and from the id. In one master metaphor (the Royal Road) Freud bypassed any possibility that the dream might serve any other than a repressive function. But Freud can be distinguished from most of his followers by his immense fascination and respect for the "genius" of the dream and what he referred to as its extraordinary artwork. As a result, *The Interpretation of Dreams* is a fundamental education in the dream process, regardless of the view one takes of the dream's function. But after Freud the dream is defined only by what it carries with it, as one might define the bloodstream as the carrier of whatever substances one might inject into it. As a consequence, most people believe that the function of the dream is to be the bearer of meanings that are somehow withheld from the dreamer but available to a skilled professional. Obviously dreams can be used successfully in an analytic capacity, but this tells us nothing about the dream itself, inasmuch as many impersonal tools of analysis serve virtually the same diagnostic purpose.

Dreams have something to do with the preservation of experience in patterns of association that pertain, in complex and as yet undefined ways, to our survival in waking reality. Dreams are not intended for our conscious understanding, and the alternative implication is not that they are mechanisms designed to censor it. Whatever dreams are doing for us, they do without our intervention or interpretation. Clearly this thesis cannot be proven at this point, and certainly not by a dreaming literary critic who stands more in awe than in understanding of advancements made in brain science. But I see signs that it is a thesis whose time may be arriving, and in the slowly expanding gyre of our interdisciplinary mood, with some luck, we may soon find ourselves in a position to look cooperatively at the dream from a fresh point of view. In the meantime, this book is a provisional step in a rhetorical direction.[11]

[11]Most notably, J. Allan Hobson's *The Dreaming Brain* (New York: Basic Books, 1988) sets forth essentially the same position as my own from a biological or psychophysiological perspective. Hobson's theory of activation-synthesis offers the most thorough scientific challenge to the notion that dreams are a mechanism of distortion and censorship. They are, rather, "transparent and unedited" (p. 12) and are in no way divided between a manifest and a latent content. Dreams, he suggests, are multifunctional and are concerned, among other things, with the "active maintenance of many brain circuits," "the consolidation of memory traces and comparison of old and new information" (p. 299) and are "fundamentally artistic" in that they use our memory of experience "to create pictures of the world against which [the brain] can test reality" (p. 297). Unfortunately, Hobson's book appeared when my own was in press and I have not been able to profit by its authority in making my case for an expressive theory of dreams. This is the case, as well, with Israel Rosenfield's *The Invention of Memory: A New View of the Brain* (New York: Basic Books, 1988), which briefly applies Gerald Edelman's theory of Darwinian memory to the dream (p. 184) and advances a theory of memory classification that has much in common with my own metaphorical theory of dreaming.

PART ONE

THE DREAM WORLD

1 *I Think, Therefore I Dream*

W E HAVE ALWAYS assumed that dreams constitute an act of speech. Because the dream, unlike other body activities, uses speech and imagery it must therefore be speaking to someone—the self to itself, the god to his prophet, the dead to the living, or even (in premonitory dreams) the future to the present. In short, dreams make sense, if one has the code to figure it out. Freud offered the most stunning code of all in his theory of wish fulfillment and repressed sexual memory, and because the shapes of the world are infinitely tolerant of sexual interpretation we have carried this code through dozens of variations and amendments before suspecting that it may have its limitations. But it is now possible to ask if we have not been making a mistake all these years. Might it be that the dream, whatever its diagnostic values, is not an act of speech in which the unconscious cryptically speaks the unspeakable to the conscious mind, but a process by which the brain maintains its operational efficiency in a world that is constantly bombarding it with experience?

In substance, this is the theory that is gradually emerging in experimental psychology and neuroscience. It is most fully exemplified by the work of the psychologist and computer scientist Christopher Evans, who suggests that in dream sleep the brain is "continually updating its vast library of [survival] programs."[1] In its primary function the dream is not speaking, it is simply working. If it is still saying things about us while it works, that is because now and then we are overhearing them as they travel along the busy circuits of the brain. Actually, Evans is not concerned with the language factor of dreams. This is an inference that I draw by extension from his theory, which seems to be the most provocative adjustment of our perspective on dreaming in the post-Freud era. My interest here has mainly to do with applications of Evans' theory that rightfully did not concern him. Primarily, these relate not to the possible functions dreams may have in the fulfillment of our psychic life, but to the phenomenal character of dreams and to the links between the imaginative processes of dreaming and those of art-making. The links between art and dreaming are very strong, but the connections we have made have been vague and analogical, beginning with the notion that in the dream state the mind somehow divides itself into a playwright-audience-participant arrangement whereby the dreamer writes the play, produces it, stars in it, and sees it on a wraparound screen in the head, all at the same time—an impressive trick by waking standards. Among other things, Evans' theory might help us temper the extravagance of this metaphor.

Evans begins by reversing one of Freud's major assumptions. Freud supposed that the purpose of the dream was

[1]Christopher Evans, *Landscapes of the Night: How and Why We Dream,* ed. Peter Evans (New York: Viking, 1983), p. 217. Throughout this book, I use the word "brain" when I refer to "the convoluted mass of nervous substance contained in the skull . . . , the organ of thought, memory, or imagination" (*The Compact Edition of the Oxford English Dictionary,* 1982 ed., definition 1) and the word "mind" when I refer to "the action or state of thinking about something" (ibid., def. 7).

to shield the sleeper from alarming thoughts and thereby preserve sleep. Evans' theory, based on an accumulation of several decades of neurophysiological research, puts it the other way: it is the function of sleep to give the brain time to dream. We do not sleep simply because we are fatigued or because the world runs, out of habit, on the rhythm of day-labor and night-rest, but because we need time to process the tremendous amount of information absorbed during the day. If the brain is anything like its progeny the computer, there is only one way this can be done, and for all organisms it is a high-risk proposition. The organism must temporarily become defenseless against its enemies. It must shut out all incoming data—go off line, as computer people say—while the brain sorts and stores the day's sensory experience in its memory banks, correlates it with earlier storage (short-term memory with long-term memory), and updates its programs, including elementary programs dealing with social conduct, skills, manners, preparations (or rehearsals) for possible conflicts to come and, more urgent, conflicts that have already arrived. In short, we need sleep so that the brain can enter the day in its ledgers, somewhat as a bank draws its shades in mid-afternoon so that the bankers can tally the day's transactions without the annoyance of customer demands.

What then is a dream? What we think of as a dream is only a fractional amount of all these operations the brain performs when it asks the body to close its doors on the world. A dream, in Evans' words, is "a momentary interception by the conscious mind [while asleep] of material being sorted, scanned, sifted, or whatever" (p. 141) during (REM) sleep. This sorting process may even extend into non-REM sleep,[2] but the dreams we experience during

[2]See, e.g., David Foulkes, "Dream Reports from Different Stages of Sleep," *Journal of Abnormal and Social Psychology* 65 (1962):14–25, and

sleep represent only a glimmer of the dream-work being carried on in the brain's banks. This work can be detected only by the waves that appear on the electroencephalogram (EEG). Many of these dreams will be forgotten on waking, but the chances that they will be recalled are highest if the dreamer is awakened when the REM activity indicates that a dream is in progress. That we forget most of our dreams—and some of us do not even remember dreaming—suggests that most dreams are not primarily of any conscious value to the dreamer, or at least they are not hieroglyphic messages but a series of hierarchical thought processes occurring on several levels of brain activity. Some of these processes are apparent, some are not. But the old concept of a resting brain has been discarded. The brain's activity, as measured by various concurrent waves, appears to be just as intense in sleep as in the waking state.

William Dement, "An Essay on Dreams: The Role of Physiology in Understanding Their Nature," in *New Directions in Psychology* (New York: Holt, 1965), 2:135–257. REM sleep, or Rapid Eye Movement sleep, often called paradoxical sleep, is sleep accompanied by darting of the eyes and an increase of heart and respiratory rates and blood flow. This is the state of sleep in which dreams, or most dreams, occur and in which neuronal activity reaches its closest approximation to the waking state. NREM sleep, or "deep sleep," is governed by neuronal regularity and a relative absence of images and dreams.

—Definitions of dreams vary widely, and from the scientific viewpoint one's definition will determine what kinds of nocturnal sensory and nonsensory experiences are admissible as dreams. In his "Essay on Dreams," Dement debates the various definitions that have been offered (pp. 184–197). My own definition is relatively simple: A dream is any series of thoughts and sensations, however brief, that is attended by visual imagery during sleep. This may be unreliable for clinical studies of the dreaming activity, and certainly for the dreams of congenitally blind people (who do not experience visual images in their dreams), but my approach is principally phenomenological, or what we might refer to as dreamer-response oriented.

So if dreams were primarily instruments of communication, most dreams would be useless, somewhat like talking into a dead telephone. Moreover, some theorists (Ramon Greenberg, for example) think that remembered dreams are failures, problems involving strong tensions that the brain could not solve. Presumably, then, successful dreams would be the dreams we do not even know we had, or remember only as a blur. A corollary to this theory is the fact that people deprived of sleep soon show acute psychological distress and when permitted to sleep they immediately increase the amount of REM sleep, and apparently the dreaming that it signals, until they are back on track.

The most intriguing support for the Evans theory comes out of the research of the French neurophysiologist Michel Jouvet. Jouvet surgically modified the brains of experimental animals so that their muscles, normally deactivated in sleep, continued to respond to the brain's instructions during the sleep state. In their REM sleep, cats suddenly jerked to life and began performing (though in a random manner) the distinctive predation movements of all cats—stalking, crouching, and springing at imaginary prey (p. 151). Even well-fed domestic cats performed the same exercises. The obvious conclusion is that the cats were dreaming of hunting and that this is probably a high-priority dream program of cats in which they rehearse their roles and sharpen the tools of food-gathering. It goes without saying that Jouvet could not extend his findings to human dreamers, but one might infer that our predation dreams simply involve more complex techniques of survival and adjustment. Dreams, then, would be useful in the sustaining way that practice is useful to the pianist, the tennis player, and the boxer, who keep in shape by playing "as if" games in preparation for the real games to come.

To me Evans' theory is welcome not because I am con-

vinced it is correct (how could any dream theory be ver-
ified?) but because it offers such a promising alternative to
our received theory of dreams. Let us consider one major
adjustment in our thinking that the Evans theory may
offer—the idea that dreams emerge from a region of the
brain called the *unconscious*. Evans does not deal much with
the unconscious except in brief discussions of Freud and
Jung, and there is some indication that he subscribes to the
idea that the unconscious does exist (p. 100). But Evans'
theory, unlike most, puts us in a position to question the
role that the unconscious may play in dreams. It would be
pointless to debate here the existence or the nature of
something as remote from observation and diversely understood as the unconscious. I am interested only in the
question of whether dreams are the manifestation of repressed desires or whether they may be explained, as I
believe they can, as aspects of expressive thought, and
perhaps the form of thought that is precisely the most free
from repression. In order to make any sense out of this
idea, it is necessary to confront the theory of the unconscious in what is certainly its most prevalent form—the
notion that the unconscious is a brain within a brain, a
psychic entity with an independent power of thought. In
the interest of brevity, I follow the argument of D. B.
Klein, who follows William James.

Klein suggests that the unconscious is an invention
rather than a discovery. We have patterned our notion of
the unconscious—at least popularly—after what we know
about the conscious mind, just as we pattern our ideas
about God after what we know about ourselves. In sum,
we have made the unconscious in our own image; we have
given it the status of a consciousness within a consciousness that is inaccessible simply because it is beneath cognitive understanding, speaking only through its affects,
and protected, like Kafka's law, by all sorts of powerful

doorkeepers posted at the preconscious border (repression, the censor, displacement, etc.). The dream's symbols and images, then, would be symptoms of the wishes and directives of the unconscious that the dreamer may not understand but that the interpreter may decode and thereby peer into that uncivil realm peopled by drives and presided over by the monstrous id. The dream is the false-hieroglyphic text that makes sense only if you presume that it is coded, and the idea of a code suggests that something with an independent intelligence has done the coding for some purpose. Hence, the dream is never what it appears to be. It is always, as Freud says, a wolf in sheep's clothing.[3]

In place of the unconscious, Klein would put nonsensory or imageless thinking. Put simply, this is thinking we do not know we are doing because it offers no signs of itself. For example, as I write, many of the words come as fast as I can put them on paper. But frequently I reach an impasse. I do not know how to say what I want to say next. I look out the window, I pace the floor, a telephone call interrupts my interruption. Eventually I get back to work, and suddenly—if I am lucky—an image, a connection, or the right word will have arrived, though I am not aware of having consciously conceived it in my ruminations. This experience is common in any problem-solving situation, and it simply means that the brain is working at the nonsensory level. Klein is arguing that what we call the unconscious consists in this kind of thinking. It is as unmysterious as a librarian searching for your book in the stacks. The unconscious is any mental activity we perform unconsciously. "But," says Klein. "this is not the same as a separate or segregated mental realm in the form of an

---

[3]Sigmund Freud, *The Standard Edition of the Complete Psychological Works of Sigmund Freud,* trans. James Strachey (London: Hogarth, 1957), 4:183. Hereafter cited as *SE.*

unconscious mind conceived of as divorced from another mental realm in the form of a conscious mind":[4]

> The concept of non-sensory ideation as a synonym for reflection, thinking, judging, and other cognitive processes suggests the unity of mental life. It does away with the notion of man being endowed with *two* minds, namely a conscious mind and an unconscious mind. It also dispenses with a not uncommon tendency to personify or reify the unconscious into some sort of spectral homunculus or psychic entity controlling the content of dreams, initiating blunders of speech and action, and even solving problems while the conscious mind is asleep (p. 215).

The notion that the unconscious is a "spectral homunculus" or even a discrete region of the brain is not held by many brain specialists. But one encounters the metaphor of the homunculus, or something like it, often enough in both clinical and literary commentary to suggest that it has some force, if only as an unexamined assumption. In typical usage, it is something less than an anatomical fact and more than a verbal convenience. In fact, in most writing there is a remarkable absence of interest in what the unconscious may be. It is mentioned as if it were, like life itself, a self-evident given. When Freud established the concept of the unconscious, he was careful to say that it was not a *place,* but still it has achieved that status. In one sense it is only a metaphorical place, but in another sense it is not. We know that as a metaphor wears out and dies it has a way of gaining a fossil reality. As John Searle points out, it is the dead metaphors that live on: "They have become

[4]D. B. Klein, *The Unconscious: Invention or Discovery? A Historico-Critical Inquiry* (Santa Monica: Goodyear, 1977), pp. 216–217.

dead through continual use, but their continual use is a clue that they satisfy some semantic need."[5] So what begins as a resemblance ends as a subtle alteration in our perception. And when we say that something "takes place" in the unconscious part of the mind is making a kind of empirical leap. Simply thinking about the unconscious is much like thinking about the basement when you are in a room upstairs.

It would be absurd to deny the existence of the unconscious on the homuncular basis alone. For example, Paul Ricoeur warns against the "naive realism" of thinking of the unconscious as "some fanciful reality with the extraordinary ability of thinking in place of consciousness."[6] Instead, the unconscious is simply "the id and nothing but the id." The id does not think, and it can be known only by the images or ideas it produces, and this implies that "someone other" than the possessor of the unconscious—the interpreter—must decipher it "through a hermeneutics which its own consciousness cannot perform alone" (p. 106). Thus the unconscious is something that seems to have only psychoanalytic actuality, a possibility suggested by Jacques Lacan as well.[7] "The fundamental meaning of the unconscious," Ricoeur says, "is in fact that an understanding always comes out of *preceding* figures, whether one understands this priority in a purely temporal and factual or symbolic sense. Man is the only being who is subject to his childhood. He is that being whose childhood constantly draws him backwards. The unconscious is thus

[5]John R. Searle, "Metaphor," in *Metaphor and Thought,* ed. Andrew Ortony (Cambridge: Cambridge University Press, 1986), p. 98.

[6]Paul Ricoeur, *The Conflict of Interpretations: Essays in Hermeneutics,* ed. Don Ihde (Evanston, Ill.: Northwestern University Press, 1974), p. 107.

[7]See Stephen Melville, "Psychoanalysis and the Place of *Jouissance,*" *Critical Inquiry* 13 (Winter 1987):365.

the principle of all regressions and all stagnations" (p. 113).

For Ricoeur, then, the unconscious would seem to be something—a history of "the figures of the spirit" (p. 120)—that is available only to a methodology. It is not in itself a psychological entity, but the path of all regression; it is "the hinterside fate of childhood and of symbols already there and reiterated, the fate of the repetition of the same themes on different helices of a spiral" (p. 118). Ricoeur goes on to say, "This is not easy to understand, and I myself do so only with difficulty" (p. 118), to which I must add my own puzzlement. However, it is not my intention here to prove or disprove either Ricoeur or the idea of the unconscious in any of its hermeneutic forms. But even if we grant the existence of the id in this or any other manifestation, or, even more plausibly, the idea of an endless regression of preceding figures that constitutes what we cannot know about ourselves, we have no proof that the mechanism of dreams is designed to conceal the desires born of this "hinterside fate." Inescapably, dreams are intimately bound up in this history of returns to "the same themes," and of this each night's dreams give us fresh proof. Where I part company with Ricoeur and most psychoanalytic theory of dreams is on the issues of repression and distortion, which have their origin in the idea of the unconscious. Let us begin with the problem of distortion, since it is the dominant affective symptom of repression.

In several respects, one cannot deny that dreams are distortions. As Ricoeur says, dreams are already a distortion in the very transposition of "desires into images."[8] In this sense all representation is distortion at the very ground

[8]Paul Ricoeur, *Freud and Philosophy: An Essay on Interpretation,* trans. Denis Savage (New Haven: Yale University Press, 1972), p. 92.

of individual perception. But, more important, one of the fundamental features of the dream is that it offers not a copy of our experience but a reconstitution of it, and therefore, again, at its origin the dream is a mechanism of distortion—that is, a mechanism that "falsifies" the experience we have lived through because it does not render it as a probable structure or a faithful account of events. The question one might pose as this level of the problem is: What character would a dream assume if it were *not* a distortion? Would it then tell "the truth" in the sense of presenting what actually happened in the dreamer's experience, at least as it is remembered? This would imply the absurdity that the dream was a kind of involuntary autobiographer. But the dream image is always a compromise with the diversity of the dreamer's history, a point that Freud makes repeatedly. Still another dimension of distortion occurs at what we may call the *inattentive level* of brain activity in the dream state. By this I mean the absence during sleep of the factor of attention, or in Jean-Pierre Changeux's words, that "essential regulatory mechanism which manages the relationship of the brain with the environment." In other words. when we are asleep the brain is not focused on a behavioral objective in the open world. Its thought, Changeux says, takes on some of the characteristics of delirious speech; words, ideas, and images are "strung together in an illogical way. . . . A *random component* appears."[9] But, he suggests, this randomness might have something to do with the way the brain processes mental events. "Could it serve to 'rehearse' mental objects and patterns so that they will not be lost during the night? Could it be responsible for continuing during sleep the stabilization of neuronal graphs begun during the day" (p.

[9]Jean-Pierre Changeux, *Neuronal Man: The Biology of Mind,* trans. Laurence Garey (New York: Pantheon, 1985), pp. 153–154.

153)? To put it another way, if the dream did not "distort," if it represented people, places, and ideas just as they are remembered from waking experience, its operations would be out of character with all the other mechanisms of storage and correlation by which the brain readies the organism for the next variation of past experience.

But none of this is what is meant by distortion in the psychoanalytic sense. Distortion, as Ricoeur says, is "the *violence done to meaning* . . . : distortion is the effect, censorship is the cause."[10] This returns us to the linguistic factor of dreams, and before continuing I want to clarify the nature of my belief that dreams do not constitute a language. It is not that I feel dreams cannot be interpreted, or that dream-reports (all we possess of dreams) are anything but a linguistic residue of the dream, or that one can discuss dreams by any other than linguistic means, or finally that speech itself is not a significant feature of dreams. Moreover, it is certainly true that in saying that dreams are expressive, rather than repressive, I appear to be claiming a certain linguistic competence for them. What I mean by "expressive," however, is not that dreams speak for our benefit but that they manifest, or make visible, something taking place in thought. One might speak, for example, of something expressing itself by simply *being* itself, without striving to communicate its being to others. Expressiveness implies, in Charles Rycroft's phrase, an "innocence of dreams," and I shall define this more carefully as the discussion proceeds. But to think of the dream as being a language in the sense of a form of speaking (as I think Rycroft does) is quite different. It implies all the assumptions of speech acts—speaker-hearer, sign-referent, signifier-signified, discourse-meaning, and so on.

I can illustrate the point best by turning directly to

[10]Ricoeur, *Freud and Philosophy,* p. 92. Ricoeur's emphasis.

Rycroft's theory of dreams, which is quite congenial with my own. For example, Rycroft believes that dreams are expressions of imaginative activity and entirely free of repression and that therefore the concept of the unconscious is "unnecessary, redundant, scientistic, and hypostasizing" because it "insinuates the idea that there really is some entity somewhere that instigates whatever we do unconsciously, some entity which is not the same entity as instigates whatever we do consciously."[11] However, because "all psychologies that attribute meaning to dreams have to postulate the existence of two selves" (one "restricted to what we know of ourselves when awake . . . , and another which embraces the whole of the personality, including that part of ourselves that dreams") (p. 66), Rycroft sees dreaming as "a private, self-to-self communication" (p. 72). "Dreams are messages from parts of the self of which the waking self is unaware, or from a more total self which the waking self cannot embrace" (p. 106): "Dreaming is thus a form of communicating or communing with oneself and is analogous to such waking activities as talking to oneself, reminding oneself, exhorting oneself, consoling oneself, frightening oneself, entertaining oneself or exciting oneself with one's own imagination—and, perhaps more particularly, to such waking meditative imaginative activities as summoning up remembrance of things past or envisaging the prospect of things future" (p. 45).

Much of this is very attractive. But it seems to me that Rycroft has thrown out the unconscious in one form only to admit it in another, though in his conception it would probably be more appropriate to call it a superconscious. My problem, however, is not with the notion of two, or several, dimensions of self-awareness, but with the notion

[11]Charles Rycroft, *The Innocence of Dreams* (New York: Pantheon, 1979), p. 19.

The Dream World

of self-to-self communication. Perhaps it comes down to this question: If I am thinking, or communing with myself, am I also communicating? Is there a center from which self-communication originates and a terminus where it is received? Let us take three analogical examples of self-communication in waking activity:

A. I hear a sound like a telephone ringing and I think, "I must remember to call Paul."
B. I am standing on the rim of the Grand Canyon and I think, "My God, that's deep!"
C. I am listening to my car radio and I hear the strain of a Glenn Miller melody. I am carried back to a high school dance in the gym.

The first example seems much like self-communication. I am virtually hanging a memo on the wall of my brain ("Call Paul"). But am I communicating with another part of myself—say, an efficient self communicating with a forgetful self? If we are to call this self-communication at all, or even simply communication, it can only be in the figurative sense. It is not as if my superego were trying to get my ego to make the telephone call. What is happening is that all-there-is-of-me, so to speak, is trying to get all-there-*will-be*-of-me to call Paul when I am next near a phone. There is no self-division or, in any real sense, self-communication involved. There is only thought, all of the brain thinking to a particular end, although thought is considerably more complex than the simple language statement "Call Paul." And likewise in the second example I could certainly be said to be speaking "to" myself, though would it not be simpler to say that I am myself speaking—that is, I am vertiginously moved to an utterance ("My God, that's deep!") that requires neither reception nor response? When speaker and listener collapse into

28

a single agent, can we speak of communication in any but a metaphorical sense? Finally, in the third example we reach something like a daydream in which I am, as it were, in two "places" at once. But again, if this imaginative division can be said to involve two parts of the self, there seems to be very little left in the realm of imaginative activity, or thought itself, that emanates from what we may call a unified self.

Rycroft's distinction is made between the waking and the dreaming self, whereas my examples pertain only to waking thought. But I see no reason to assume that dreams, because they appear to be occurring independently of my control or because they seem to be relevant to my experience, should be considered as instances of self-to-self communication, at least in normal circumstances. It is quite possible that in the case of severely disturbed people (whom psychoanalysts regularly deal with) the dream mechanism might also be disturbed and assume, so to speak, a split personality that seems to be sending messages to the dreamer. Like the body itself, dreams might manifest different or additional characteristics in the case of people being treated for psychoses. I have no experience in these matters. I am simply holding the view that if dreams mean anything they do not *mean* to mean anything, and that the clinical act of retrieval of meaning does not imply that dreams are telling the dreamer something he needs to know about himself or preventing him from finding out something that might disturb his sleep. In saying this, I do not want to give the impression that Rycroft is falling into the fallacy of a homuncular "superconscious." I suspect that some of the problem may be with the language one is forced to use in discussing the way meaning actually *means,* in and out of dreams, and that Rycroft has set up something analogous to a model, like Bohr's model of the atom as a miniature solar system—it is *wrong,* but it is at least a way of giving body to something we cannot hope to see. In any case, the self-communication model is problematical. If Rycroft were referring only to a dialectical habit of thought whereby one debates the opposing sides of an issue "with oneself" or is "of two minds" (i.e., indecisive) about something, I would have no problem. These are simply the quandaries that come with solving problems and making choices of all kinds. It also seems possible that the dream state, because of its isolation from the immediate concerns of social orientation and its intensified metaphorical capability, may have a greater access to the overall materials of the dreamer's experience. In other words, one might learn something about oneself from dreams. But I believe Rycroft is implying something firmer—that dreams, on some level, speak intentionally—and that takes us back, or toward, a two-mind system that is scarcely an improvement over the homuncular unconscious: dreams are messages, communications—and communication by any definition implies a sender, a medium, and a receiver. Dreams, Ricoeur says, "border on language, since they can be told, analyzed, interpreted"; "the analyst interprets [the dreamer's] account, substituting for it another text which is, in his eyes, the thought-content of desire, i.e. what desire would say could it speak without restraint."[12] So it is not the dream that does the speaking; it is the dreamer, or rather the ex-dreamer, an unwitting patient who "delivers" his mute illness to his physician in hope of getting a diagnostic translation.

Here we arrive at the peculiar value that dreams have in the clinical situation: a dream is a Rorschach blot in narrative form that is endlessly useful because it is, as Rycroft says, "open to interpretation" (p. 162). This is basically

---

[12]Ricoeur, *Freud and Philosophy,* p. 15.

the ground on which Ludwig Wittgenstein complained about Freud's interpretive method: it would work as well on a random collection of objects on a table.[13] But from a purely diagnostic standpoint, this complaint is all but irrelevant because it is not what has been put into the dream that matters, but what one can get out of it. For example, suppose I steal someone else's dream and take it, as my own, to my analyst for interpretation. The dream begins, let us say, in the square of a small town and soon moves to a forest, where I am walking with a woman I do not know. There are many animals around us, and presently a unicorn joins us as we walk toward a clearing. Although I am being untruthful in saying that it is my dream, I honestly try to tell the analyst what it brings to my mind from my own emotional experience. This presents no difficulty because my own small town had a square, I am fond of walking in forests, and (among many other associations) I have a niece who collects unicorns. Indeed, my theft of this particular dream may have something to do with the familiarity of its plot elements. So in choosing and talking about the dream, I am automatically talking about myself. Moreover, through the principles of condensation, displacement, symbolism, and contradiction, my analyst, taking the dream on faith, has all the means for bringing it on line with my own psychological profile, as we have shared it in previous sessions.

I am not suggesting that analysts are credulous, but rather that dreams can be used as legitimate diagnostic tools whether they are true or faked. This is made possible, in part, by the adaptability of symbols—in this case, the square, forest, animals, woman, and unicorn—whose

---

[13]Ludwig Wittgenstein, *Lectures and Conversations on Aesthetics, Psychology, and Religious Beliefs,* ed. Cyril Barrett (Berkeley and Los Angeles: University of California Press, 1966), pp. 50–51.

meanings are determined by the context in which they appear. Certainly my own dreams would coincide with my psychic life far better than this unicorn dream I have paraphrased from an essay by Jean Laplanche and Serge Leclaire, which happens to be the dream of a "thirty-year-old obsessional neurotic" named Philippe.[14] Of course there is no way one could possibly tell from the details themselves who, or what sort of person (neurotic or otherwise), had dreamed this dream, and this is partly the point. In becoming reports, or texts, rather than deeply personal psychic events that occur in sleep, dreams (like Rorschach blots) are impersonal artifacts. In fact, in thinking and writing about Philippe's dream I have made it my own, for as the report passes into my mind I unavoidably visualize it—I daydream it—and though it still bears a structural resemblance to Philippe's dream, it now takes place in my town square, my forest, with my unknown woman and unicorn, all of which have been summoned to life from my unique experience with such images. Moreover, having personalized the dream, I would have little difficulty making a certain psychic sense of it because the images, thus personalized, now carry affects, or feelings (the square is inviting, ominous; the woman is seductive, mysterious, pleasant; the unicorn is friendly, hostile; and so on), that could be seen as "symbolic" of my psychic situation. In short, as a *text,* the dream belongs to no one, it has no intrinsic meaning. Whatever meaning it has must be derived circumstantially from what one knows about the dreamer's life outside the dream, or in the present case about the false dreamer who is reporting it. A dream is more a mirror than a lamp; it will reflect what one puts before it, and that is always as much the eye of the inter-

[14]Jean Laplanche and Serge Leclaire, "The Unconscious: A Psychoanalytic Study," *Yale French Studies* 48 (1972): 136.

preter as the "I" of the dreamer.[15] In this vein, one of the more fascinating branches of recent Freud study has been the reinterpretation of Freud's own dreams or, more precisely, of Freud's interpretations of his dreams. They have achieved the status of literary texts, and it is reasonable to assume that we will one day be revising these reinterpretations along new diagnostic lines. The legitimacy of such a project lies not in its objective truth but in the persuasiveness with which one can give meaning to the available "facts."

Unfortunately, as with the homuncular notion of the unconscious, this three-step diagnostic process from

---

[15]Peter Brooks' rhetorical theory of the reader-text relationship as being analogous to the analyst-analysand relationship is quite appropriate to the analysis of dreams. In reading, Brooks suggests, an act of transference and a rewriting of the text occur. "A transferential model thus allows us to take as the object of analysis not author or reader, but reading, including, of course, the transferential-interpretive operations that belong to reading" ("The Idea of a Psychoanalytic Literary Criticism," *Critical Inquiry* 13 [Winter 1987]: 345; see also Brooks' *Reading for the Plot: Design and Intention in Narrative* [New York: Random House, 1985], esp. "Narrative Transaction and Transference," pp. 216–237). Similarly, the dream is not the "object of analysis," but the site of a transference between the dreamer, and all of his past, and the analyst who intervenes in the dream, "re-constructs" it, as Brooks says of the reader-interpreter, thereby achieving "the *effect* of the real." For quite legitimate psychoanalytic purposes, then, it would not make the slightest difference whether the dream is a repression or a faithful expression of what was on the dreamer's mind. Either way, the interpretation is a revision of the dream for purposes other than understanding what, if anything, the dream may mean. It is, as Macbeth puts it, a lie *like* truth or a likeness of a truth that has no single source, or cause, or reduction to a concrete event, and therefore something that can come to light only in what is technically a falsehood. The dream becomes a kind of *pharmakos* that is sacrificed to a better understanding of "the problem," and like the *pharmakos* the dream will serve its cathartic function irrespective of its innocence or guilt—that is, whether it is interpreted "correctly" or not.

dream to dream-report to meaning tends to get short-circuited in our thinking about dreams. We think of the dream itself as doing the speaking; we attribute to it a facility bordering on intelligence that expresses itself in the obfuscation of truth. Thus we assign to the dream what belongs to the analysis. It is not that the dream and the analytical "text" may not belong to each other in a very intimate way. The question is: Need we assume that the dream's manifest character has been determined by an act of censorship whereby repressed thoughts appear in disguised form? Is it not possible that the dream is more like a truffle pig than a wolf in sheep's clothing? That is: it may *lead* to an analytical solution, but its "motive" had strictly to do with the routine correlation of significant signals from the day's experience with similar experience already stored in the long-term memory. This is the process that Stanley Palombo calls "matching,"[16] and as we shall see, it is probably much the same process that Gerald Edelman refers to as *classification* in his theory of Darwinian memory.[17]

I am suggesting, then, that what looks from one point of view like a mechanism of repression might, from another, be considered an instance of memory formation, or recall, or imaginative and constructive thought of various kinds. Of course, as Palombo maintains, it does not follow that our acceptance of the "matching" process as the primary function of dreams requires a full rejection of the censorship principle.[18] It is possible that people with con-

[16]Stanley R. Palombo, *Dreaming and Memory: A New Information-Processing Model* (New York: Basic Books, 1978), pp. 43–53 and passim.

[17]Gerald M. Edelman, "Through a Computer Darkly: Group Selection and Higher Brain Function," *Academy of Arts and Sciences Bulletin* 36 (October 1982):38.

[18]Palombo is inconclusive about the role of censorship in dreams, no doubt because "we know very little about the nature of the censorship

firmed psychoses dream differently from so-called normal people and that defense mechanisms are somehow involved in such cases. I will leave this matter to psychoanalysts. But to base a comprehensive theory of dreams on what appears to be a special condition of mental disturbance seems premature, to say the least. There is some indication, beginning with evidence from sleep clinics, that dreams have much more basic business than preventing the flow of repressed thought to the conscious mind. This view is encouraged by the fact that dreaming is widespread in the animal kingdom. What could animals possibly be repressing? And if they are repressing nothing, why has nature seen fit to endow them with the dream mechanism, unless dreams were intended (at least originally) to serve other functions that are completely unrelated to repressed infantile memory, to the protection of sleep, or to language?[19] And how can we be sure that these functions have not been continued in man, along with the accretion of newer functions arising from the discontents of civiliza-

---

mechanism"; we know "more about what censorship does than how it does it" (ibid., p. 91). In his discussion, censorship is a factor in dream formation, but chiefly in cases where "neurotic symptoms" are involved. Palombo's main emphasis is on what he calls the memory-cycle model, in which "the dream compares the representation of an emotionally significant event of the past with the representation of an emotionally significant aspect of the previous day's experience" (p. 219).

[19]One gathers that Freud's idea that dreams are the guardians of sleep has been all but discarded. Moreover, it is difficult to know how seriously Freud himself believed that the primary function of dreams was to protect sleep—for example, Richard M. Jones: "Actually, Freud seemed to regard the dream's guardianship of sleep as a mere fact and not as a hypothesis at all. The sleep-protection idea was consistent with the wish-fulfillment hypothesis because the latter carried implications of tension reduction, and sleep was then vaguely conceived as a state of reduced tension. The crucial point is that the sleep-protection hypothesis is largely independent of psychological theories of dreaming" (*The New Psychology of Dreaming* [New York: Viking, 1970], p. 41).

tion, the burdens of self-deceit, moral taboos, and so on—in short, that it is a poly-functional system rather than the single unitary system Freud claimed to have found, a system conceivably as capacious as the mind itself? It is true that we are different from the animals, but do we not need the dream for similar animal purposes?

Freud closes his chapter entitled "Dreams as Wish-Fulfillments" by saying that he does not know what animals dream of. Then he cites a proverb: "'What,' asks the proverb, 'do geese dream of?' And it replies: 'Of maize.' The whole theory that dreams are wish-fulfillments is contained in these two phrases."[20] This would be a very un-Freudian dream in its undisguised simplicity, but Freud would plausibly argue that the dreams of animals, like those of children, are more transparent and infantile than the dreams of human adults, which carry a lot more psychic freight. But one doubts that the goose would dream so innocently of maize. Even if the goose had nothing to repress, it would probably produce what Freud would call a rebus. If one could surgically activate the muscular system of the sleeping goose, one would probably find that it went through its entire maize-seeking routine in a random and disorganized—a seemingly *censored*—sequence, like Jouvet's cats. That is, it would dream not of maize itself (like the food dreams of animals we see in the cartoon thought-balloons), but of the manifold contexts in which maize, to simplify the life of the goose radically, figures as a central principle of survival—a dream of maize as an explosive collage of patterns, a network of associated neuronal graphs or programs owing nothing to goose-language and everything to the inexhaustible contingencies of barnyard life.

Let us assume that the idea of the unconscious as the site

[20]Freud, *SE* 4:131–132.

of interpretation, a linguistic locus between "the inside" and "the outside," is a tenable one. It is a hypothesis held by many intelligent people, and it has been seriously held up to such scrutiny as we are able to give the workings of the brain. Moreover, as Lacan says, if something were discovered in the place of the unconscious "it would be quite immaterial" because the unconscious, at least for Freud, is simply "that point where . . . there is always something wrong."[21] But now let us ask, If we do away with the idea of the unconscious as a separate region of the brain, what have we lost? We have not done away with drives or neuroses or complexes or repression itself; we have simply demystified the activity of the brain by releasing it from a secret spatial and self-competitive division. And in doing away with the two-mind system, we find that there is no reason to explain the distortions of dreams as products of displacement and censorship.

We are now in a position to see that everything that takes place in the dream is an activity of cooperative thought, much of which (as in waking life) falls beneath sensory awareness. Moreover, the concept of nonimagistic thought helps us deal with the problem of how we can dream without experiencing the dream or remembering that we have dreamed. Whereas Freud would say that such dreams are not forgotten but simply repressed, we would claim that—if indeed they can be called dreams—they are simply unfolding at a meta-imagistic level of thought. They are not quite dreams, or not yet dreams. We can only speculate on what such thought might be about or what form it may take, but a great deal of the sorting, scanning, and processing of data that Evans discusses might be occurring at this level. It is interesting to note that, in the

[21]Jacques Lacan, *The Four Fundamental Concepts of Psycho-analysis,* trans. Alan Sheridan (New York: Norton, 1981), p. 22.

foreword to Klein's book *The Unconscious,* Judd Marmor expresses a wish that Klein "had elaborated to a greater extent on information theory and the concept of the brain as a processor and storer of data." To me the remark suggests the affinity between Evans' computer-dream theory and Klein's theory of nonsensory ideation. In fact, if we fuse the findings of the Evans and Klein books we get a much clearer sense of the possible relationship between dreaming and thinking of all kinds. A dream, or what we think of as a dream, may simply be one kind of nocturnal thinking, just as the daydream is one kind of diurnal thinking. Being both imagistic and auditory, a dream is the part of ideation that lies nearest to cognitive, or "finished," thinking. This does not mean that it is more rational, only that it is more a perceptual phenomenon. We might think of a dream as being like a resistance in a circuit or like a seismographic excitation of the smooth flow of non-imagistic processing. Finding ourselves, as we invariably do, *in medias res* in our dreams ("I was in this room . . .") might be the result of nonsensory thought gradually converting itself into a dream. In this connection, it might be a helpful analogy to recall something Kierkegaard said about Socratic thought, which frequently interrupts its dialectical procedures with a myth. When dialectic fails to solve the problem, we resort to the mythical, which, Kierkegaard says, is addressed not to the understanding but to the imagination. "In the mythical representation," he goes on, "both time and space have only imaginary reality."[22] In the mythical portion of our thought, the poet in us "dreams into being all that the dialectician . . . sought to establish" (p. 139). This is somewhat fanciful, and I offer it not as a proof but as a way—a myth, if you will—of

[22]Søren Kierkegaard, *The Concept of Irony, with Constant Reference to Socrates,* trans. Lee M. Capel (Bloomington: Indiana University Press, 1965), p. 137n.

accounting for the onset of the dream out of nonimagistic thought.

It is a simplification to say that the dream replaces non-imagistic thought, because the mind probably continues its other work beneath the dream. One of the most fascinating aspects of dreaming is the sense of being completely within a world we have created in our own heads. In the dream I seem to be my waking self. I respond to the dream situation as I might in waking life, even to assessing the motives and intentions of other people in the dream. I think, I feel, I evaluate, I am myself. The dream has deprived me of none of my mental equipment except the ability to discern that I am using it in a situation that is not real. In lucid dreams I may even be aware of being in a dream. Within my dream, then, my nonsensory thought continues to process the visual data presented by the dream, even as the dream itself is part of the processing of the data of my real day. I have been drawn recursively into my own thought process, where I continue to think thoughts about the thoughts I am thinking in the dream-form. Thus day experience and dream experience stand in a parallel relationship as phenomena of perception; both are attended by the same subprocesses of nonperceptual or involuntary ideation that enable us, in daily life as in dreams, to adjust continually to what is happening to us. To sum up the point, the Harvard neurobiologist David Hubel offers a wonderfully succinct account of the scene in the brain: "In brief, there is an input: man's only way of knowing about the outside world. There is an output: man's only way of responding to the outside world and influencing it. And between input and output there is everything else, which must include perception, emotions, memory, thought and whatever else makes man human.[23]

[23]David H. Hubel, "The Brain," *Scientific American* 241 (September 1979): 50. This is an appropriate place to mention Gerald Edelman's

39

But where to put the dream—is it output or input? It is certainly a reaction to the world's input, something the brain does by way of response to experience and therefore an output of a sort. But this output has the virtually unique characteristic of reducing the world's input to still another world, remade in its own image, that becomes in effect a recycled input, a twice-told tale, to which we as dreamer have a sensory rereaction that is approximately like our reaction to the world.

Where dreaming is concerned, all theorists are in the situation of the blind men and the elephant. There can be no scientific theory of dreams beyond the neurophysiological phase or beyond a certain more-or-less observable relationship between dreaming and neural excitation. All

---

reservations about the brain-computer analogy ("Through a Computer Darkly: Group Selection and Higher Brain Function," *Academy of Arts and Sciences Bulletin* 36 [October 1982]: 20–49). The brain, Edelman says, does not work like a computer. It "does not store information in a particular location as the computer does, and [it] does not replicate information exactly" (p. 41). Moreover, the difficulty with the computer analogy "has to do not so much with the theory of computation as with the famous ghost that haunts all considerations of the brain, namely, the homunculus. Who, in fact, is telling whom what to do? Who is writing the program?" (p. 22). In Edelman's view, the brain is a Darwinian mechanism that evolves as a highly variable selective system "during the worldly sojourn" of the individual (p. 22). "There is no god in this machine," he says, "there is no telegrapher, no programmer, and no homunculus" (p. 43), and presumably no unconscious, or at least I do not see how Edelman's theory of the brain could accommodate the notion of anything like an unconscious in the psychoanalytic meaning of the term. In any case, we should keep his argument in mind when we think of the brain as being in any sense like a computer. The brain is *a kind of* computer in that it is a mechanism for processing and storing information, but at the very least we can say that it stores and retrieves information in different ways and for different purposes. For other comparisons between the brain and the computer, see Changeux's *Neuronal Man,* pp. 126–127, and F. H. C. Crick, "Thinking about the Brain," *Scientific American* 241 (September 1979):219–232.

hypotheses about dreams are unavoidably built on the personal memory of the ex-dreamer and the dream memories of other ex-dreamers, and this guesswork is compounded because we recall only shards of dreams. In other words, an interpretation of a dream is a translation of a partial translation (the dream-report) of an imitation (the dream itself) of something that apparently began as a thought or a feeling that took form in the neocortex as a consequence of the organism's experience. Nevertheless, in this impossible predicament, and with far less temerity than my tone may suggest, I want to advance several postulates that emerge from the Evans and Klein investigations.

First, *the dream does not disguise.* It is just what it is—one of the bluntest of psychic experiences. It suppresses nothing, neither images of death, lust, or incest, nor the pain of humiliation or loss, nor the repugnance of excrement and filth, any one of which might awaken one in shock. Moreover, the dream may pass over a pressing fear the dreamer has taken to sleep, and one might have a pleasant dream (a wish fulfillment perhaps?) on the eve of one's execution. Dreams, Jung says, "are a part of nature, which harbors no intention to deceive, but expresses something as best it can."[24] This view is apparently becoming more and more attractive to dream specialists as the functional similarities between brain and computer are more closely studied. For example, in *Brain and Psyche* Jonathan Winson endorses the computer theory of dreaming. While he holds to Freud's idea of the unconscious, it is not as the dark house of the id but as the nerve center of the brain's processing of information. Winson's unconscious, moreover, is quite close to Klein's nonsensory thinking, and it may be all but academic whether we throw out Freud's unconscious, as Klein

[24]Carl G. Jung, *Memories, Dreams, Reflections,* trans. Richard and Clara Winston, ed. Aniela Jaffe (New York: Random House, 1965), pp. 161–62.

suggests, or revise and retain it along Winson's lines: "I believe that the phylogenetically ancient mechanisms involving REM sleep, in which memories, associations, and strategies are formed and handled by the brain as a distinct category of information in the prefrontal cortex and associated structures, are in fact the Freudian unconscious."[25] For Winson, dreams are "a window on the neural process," and it is a matter of chance that we are aware of them at all, and perhaps irrelevant whether we remember them or forget them on waking. Thus dream distortion is not a defense mechanism but "a reflection of the normal associative process by which experience is interpreted and integrated" (p. 214).

Perhaps the so-called distortion of dreams is best accounted for by the phenomenon of "inner speech," which is treated in detail by Heinz Werner and Bernard Kaplan. Inner speech is "self-directed" speech, as opposed to external speech, which is communal or other-directed. I would also distinguish it from self-to-self communication in that it presupposes no self-division or hierarchy of self-awareness. Inner speech reaches its "extreme condition" in the dream where all speakers, listeners, and images are supplied, so to speak, by the dreaming self.[26] As a result, dream–speech is apt to occur at a level of "subcodification": connotations of words are diffuse and interwoven, syntax is abbreviated, logical connections are not articulated, neologisms are common, and meanings are personalized. The notion of inner speech in dreams does not preclude the possibility of dream conversations making

[25]Jonathan Winson, *Brain and Psyche: The Biology of the Unconscious* (Garden City, N.Y.: Doubleday, 1985), p. 209.

[26]See Heinz Werner and Bernard Kaplan, *Symbol Formation: An Organismic-Developmental Approach to Language and the Expression of Thought* (New York: Wiley, 1963), p. 241.

sense. It is quite possible to use external speech lucidly in a dream, at least in brief stretches, just as it is possible to make inner-speech "mistakes" when you are awake (e.g., unintentional puns, syllable reversals). But the phenomenon accounts for the tendency of dreams to speak "in tongues" foreign to waking grammar and logic. This is what makes it possible to have an "intelligent" conversation in a dream that is, by the standards of external speech, pure nonsense. My dream-companion understands exactly what I mean when I say "Grandma is in the organhorse drembling" because he is not so much hearing my words as reading my mind—or should I say *our* mind? In many respects, inner speech is virtually identical to imagination, though Werner and Kaplan do not use that word. It is a form of thinking—need we restrict it, in fact, to speech?—that enables the brain to avoid "unnecessary redundancy and facilitate rapidity of thinking" (p. 323) and to make original leaps over the bounded world of predefined things and ideas. Moreover, at this level of thought it is difficult to separate speech from imagery, for it is characteristic of dream speech to become fused with things or to disappear entirely into an image: "Verbal conceptions are easily transformed into concrete images, and images are quickly 'translated' into verbal expressions. In other words, the various media which are relatively segregated from each other on the level of communication to others are, in the dream, interwoven with each other and with ongoing bodily states" (p. 243).

I suggest that this is the true basis of so-called dream distortion and, by extension, of dream disguise and censorship. Freud says that distortion and censorship "correspond down to their smallest details" and that this "justifies us in presuming that they are similarly determined."[27]

---

[27]Freud, *SE* 4:143.

But what Freud's examples show is a correspondence between dream "distortion" and his own interpretations rather than a possible censorship. In other words, in interpreting a dream one necessarily translates it out of what it is into something it connotatively corresponds to. An interpretation will therefore always be different from the dream (or a literary text), but this does not mean that the difference constitutes a censorship or that the dream is a distortion. Distortion is simply the process of symbol formation taking place beneath articulated speech and meaning where polysemantic and dystaxic structures are perfectly normal. To say that dreams distort reality, then, is somewhat like visiting China and describing all the people there as foreigners. If we take the dream on its own native ground, we see that it creates its world according to an *inner* principle of thought and speech that has nothing to do with our waking conceptions of reality. To sum it up in a familiar example, let us say that a married couple, on returning home in the evening, has a bitter quarrel, ending in violence and threats about divorce, over who lost the key to the front door. Here is a perfect instance of distortion if the scene were viewed from the street by a passing stranger. We would certainly say that the couple had got everything out of proportion, for the loss of a key is an absurdly inadequate cause for such a fuss. Yet if one were aware of the tensions in this marriage, one could easily trace the origin of the incident to something that had happened earlier, and most likely to a history of irritability of which the key episode was not "the key episode" at all but simply the latest point of discharge.

And this is the case with the dream image as well. It is a conducting rod for pent-up feelings for which no single image or cause can be fully expressive, at least by waking logic. The dream image is always provisional, and its "distortion" is a function of its polygeneous nature. Thus the words "You *always* say that!" which steadily creeps into the quarrels of intimates, have an analogue in the dream where we get only one image at a time but it is always generic—that is, it always carries a history of feeling and therefore is always a compromise among possible images. All in all, the presumption of distortion implies a chauvinism of the interpretive eye. Even the most innocent statement about last night's dream (for example, "For some weird reason, this monster knew exactly where I was hiding") is a falsification of the dream because it attributes to it a quality—uncanniness—that it possesses only in the light of day. Dreams are not uncanny. The monster knows where the dreamer is hiding because it is an alter ego of the dreaming self that has been deployed as menace. The dreamer may be astonished by this figura of his self, which is always *the other* in the dream, but he never doubts the normalcy of what is astonishing him. Again, a statement like "The room had no walls, but I knew it was a room" expresses only the dreamer's hopeless exile from the dream world. It drains out of the dream everything but a certain structure of unlikelihood and reduces it to a deformed *representation* of reality that is of interest only because it is implausible or uncanny. How can one capture the normality of a dream-room when the act of saying that it had no walls constitutes an awareness of abnormality (one would never say "I was in this room and it had walls")? On this ground, Kafka is one of our best dream-artists because he is so unsurprised by queerness. Like all true˙ dream-artists, Kafka understood that dream imagery is never dreamlike ("foreboding," "uncanny"); it faces the dreamer in perfect accord with its nature. Gregor Samsa awakens from "a troubled dream" to find himself "changed in his bed to some monstrous kind of vermin." The dream quality of the story, however, arises not from the impossible event (which Gregor finds a "stupidity") but from the absence of incredulity in the account. On the dreamscape, in short, we are dream-natives; its possibilities are our possibilities, a fact that is registered most clearly when we suddenly wake up from the dream and find ourselves in the alien land of the real world.

The logic of the dream, then, is not to represent or to distort a "normal" room, but to produce a space coterminous with a feeling. The dream image is half thought, or feeling, and half perceptual experience. In the dream it is possible to watch a football game between the Pittsburgh Steelers and the philosophy of Schopenhauer. Here is a personal dream that will illustrate the point more clearly:

In an inexplicit place in a forest I am having a conversation with my enemy the snake. By one of those inexplicable reversals of expectation, it wishes me no harm and I have no fear. The verbal content of our conversation is unclear, and we are apparently communicating through our eyes, in which we seem to read each other's minds. Certainly the snake does not move its lips while speaking, as it does in the cartoons, and it is not coiled up on the ground, snake-like. Indeed, it is somewhat erect, sitting in a (possible) chair. At one point, it seems to be sipping tea, but I have no idea how, since it does not seem to have arms and hands. Soon the snake becomes outgoing, and I am pleased by this. I experience intense devotion and a desire to be a friend of the snake forever. I apologize for all my past errors and crimes committed against snakes. We vow our friendship, and the snake waves goodbye and leaves.

Here, surely, is a classic wish-fulfillment dream in which I have dreamed away the enigma of the wall between the species, the terrible foreignness of the creature that has no voice or appendages. My inability to describe the snake or to explain how it does these "human" things is not the result of forgetting the details of the dream, for the dream is finally only my thought condensed and displayed as the snake. But in the graphics of dream imagery, snake and human are not two different things held together by an idea, nor do they form a single image constituted like a chimera (a snakelike man or a manlike snake). Rather, the *presence* of the snake is a kind of oscillation between essence and icon. Hence it is impossible for me to say whether the snake had legs even though it walked away. The dream image is simply a hybrid phenomenon, at once spatial and ideational, born at the point where a feeling condenses into a form, where it has no choice but to become form. The dream image does not *arouse* feeling; it is instead the feeling that arouses the image, which is so deeply saturated in the feeling that it is impossible to distinguish one from the other. This is one reason that the dream image seems so strange on recall. It has in effect become severed from its precise psychic charge, without which it is the absurd and trivial parody of reality ("I was riding through heavy traffic on my son's tricycle," "We were all sitting in this huge tree eating dinner").

The triviality and absurdity of the dream image leads us to a second postulate: *The dream selects its content algebraically from the dreamer's experience.* I have in mind here the sense of algebra as a calculus of general symbols dealing with the relations and properties of things rather than with the things themselves (arithmetic). In this respect, the dream is, as Aristotle would say, less a personal historian than a poet. It expresses not *what* happened but *the kind of thing* that has happened and can happen again, or what a happening might signify as a psychic residue. There is, therefore, at once an extratemporal or Parnassian[28] aspect

[28]Parnassian refers to the painting from the school of Parnassus in which all the philosophers in history are gathered on a single mountaintop, thus forming "a group in the conceptual sense" (*SE* 4:314).

to the dream image, together with a degree of versatility, or *x*-ness, in what it will bear. The image is to some extent a carrier on which the dream feeling rides, like a hitch-hiker. Consequently, it is unstable as an identity and dynamic as a form. The dream is capable of carrying a known and an unknown in the same image, primarily, as we shall see in Part Two, because the image is always a metaphorical construction. This split effect is what makes it possible for the dreamer to think, semilucidly, during the dream, "It is my cat, but I don't recognize it" or "It is my mother, but she is someone else." To take the more interesting case, suppose I am talking to my mother in my dream and I become vaguely aware that she has become a woman I have never seen. I go on talking to her all the same, as if she were still my mother. And she is—in principle, or rather in feeling—for I have simply transferred my feeling for my mother to the stranger woman. I am mildly confused and disappointed by this transformation, but it is forgotten as thought of my mother fades and the stranger asserts her unique personality.

What can we make of this? There is a side of my mother I do not know? I am afraid she might desert me, and my fears are realized in this incident? At the bottom of motherliness there is something alien? Is something sexual going on here? (Who *is* this stranger?) Such questions take it for granted that there is something meaningful behind this transformation; the dream is speaking in tongues. But let us suppose that this is not the case, that the feeling inhering in the event (mild disappointment) is precisely appropriate to it, and that if the feeling had been stronger (say, fear of my mother abandoning me, or even fear of incest) the dream would have pursued it openly. In other words, the transformation was not performed as a thematic act, but was the result of the dream's "normal associative process" of making images to suit its thoughts.

48

Mother had simply ceased to be relevant to the progress of the dream. Having conjured her, my dream proceeds to revise her, briefly retaining her identity but generating a new person out of some seed of association, beneath interpretation, that was suggested by her image and manner. Here we have a process that is quite normal in the waking world in which something before you reminds you of something else and for the moment you "see double." In the dream, however, there is nothing to ground your attention in the immediate reality, to call you "back," since the immediate reality is the dream itself. Because all images have the same mutable status, they float in and out of one another, at the whim of the dreaming consciousness. It is the nature of the dream image to seek and to attract other dream images. This is perfectly expressed by the dream-artist Magritte: "Likeness is not concerned with agreeing with 'common sense' or with defying it, but only with spontaneously assembling shapes from the world of appearance in an order given by inspiration."[29]

This would be unacceptable to most psychoanalytic theories of dreaming, which assume that the dream is efficient and knows exactly what it is doing. There is no such stuttering in the language of the dream. But this notion imposes a staggering and unnecessary demand on the dreamwork. It virtually presumes either that the details of the dream have been worked out in advance and stored in cassette form, as one current theory runs,[30] or that the dream has an extraordinary ability to keep ahead of its story and have the next event ready without so much as a pause in the swift current of its progress (for example, try staying on a single subject during a daydream). But the

[29]Quoted in Suzi Gablik's *Magritte* (Greenwich, Conn.: New York Graphic Society, 1971), p. 142.

[30]See Daniel C. Dennett, "Are Dreams Experiences?" *Philosophical Review* 85 (April 1976):151–171.

brain that dreams is the same brain that makes mistakes in logic, has difficulty solving perplexing problems, or is "not good" at math or at remembering names and directions. May we not assume, then, as our third postulate, that *the dream is subject to the same failures, false starts, dead ends, and errors in thought as the waking mind?* If we reflect on our own thinking—how we arrive at decisions, how we think about yesterday and today, how we browse through our life's contents while driving a car—it becomes clear that the seeming chaos of the dream is nothing very special. In normal thought we spin our wheels, make bad decisions, and bark up wrong trees. Why then should the dream, unfolding under less urgent and less attentive conditions, be any different? Or why should the dream have more meaning or order than waking thought, or be considered a more efficient mechanism of thought than the waking dream? Might it not be producing, as Jung says, "as best it can" what amounts to a first and only draft— that is, a series of images on a given theme, some of which must be amended or rejected or gradually phased out? This would appear not as a failure or a revisionary process to the dreaming consciousness, but as an experience like those of waking life—but an experience that will appear distorted or chaotic when recalled. The dream, then, is thought as it occurs, not as it has been perfected in another part of the brain and passed into the dream in a finished state, like an edited film. The dream does not have time to think because it is itself the thinking.[31]

[31]This idea runs contrary to the thesis of Jean-François Lyotard in "The Dream-Work Does Not Think" (trans. Mary Lydon), *Oxford Literary Review* 6 (1983): 3–34. Lyotard offers an elaborate revision of Freud's theory of wish fulfillment in which the dream does not fulfill a particular wish but fulfills the wish of desire, a force located in the unconscious, to cast itself on the dream-thoughts in the form of a figural image or a "violence perpetrated on linguistic space" (p. 9).

The most provocative discussion of this idea occurs in Kenneth Burke's essay "*Somnia ad Urinandum*." Burke suggests that the dream may not be repressing anything when it resorts to odd combinations of imagery and that it may not, as Jung claimed, have something "archaic" on its mind. It may simply be faced with a common problem: how to find the right word. In poetry, as in all discourse, a wide range of images and analogies can always serve to symbolize, or "sum up," any particular motive. In waking life we can refine our metaphors and symbols to a sharp edge of accuracy and expressiveness. "But in sleep," Burke says, "when the critical faculties are less exacting than during times of maximum alertness, a dreamer might be temporarily 'satisfied' with any mode of representation that remotely resembles the motive or complex of motives with which his dream happens to be preoccupied."[32] In other words, the "sheer complexity of the problem" the dream faces, and (I would add) the rapidity with which it must invent, forces it to settle (by waking standards at least) for less than perfect imagery. Dreams, like poets, nod now and then.

Burke modestly poses this idea as an "occasional cause" of the strangeness of dream symbolism, and to this degree there is no reason that it may not work cooperatively with the causes advanced by Freud and Jung (for both of whom, overall, Burke has considerable sympathies). A Freudian psychologist would probably insist that the inadequacy of the image—if he would agree in principle that it *is* inadequate—occurred in the larger and more important context of censorship and disguise. Moreover, if we dream unceasingly by day and night, as Wilhelm Stekel main-

[32]Kenneth Burke, *Language as Symbolic Action: Essays on Life, Literature, and Method* (Berkeley and Los Angeles: University of California Press, 1966), p. 345.

tained,[33] it would follow that the symbols of the dream are, or may be, carefully cured in the unconscious, much as a poet is said to "write" his poem when he isn't even thinking about it. But even if this is true, it does not dispose of Burke's thesis. Burke is suggesting that the dream may occasionally be confronted by conflicting motives— one possibly very immediate and one of longer-range (any pressing problem from the day or from life in general). Thus a dream may involve a confrontation between a physiological motive and a narrative motive. As his main example, Burke cites the problem of having to urinate while one is dreaming. We are all familiar with this sort of dream in which the "current" of the dream is suddenly (or gradually) contaminated by a urinary input and the dream must put aside its plot and find a bathroom. In short, this sudden clash of motives would confuse the dream and bring it to a crossroads from which there is no correct direction to proceed. So what may appear to be a symbol of repressed fear may really be a compromise, if not a blown fuse, brought on by an overloaded circuit.

To say that an image is bungled is not to imply that it fails as far as the dream is concerned. While Burke emphasizes that the dream symbol is inadequate as a summation of highly complex motives (a judgment made on *this* side of the dream), we might as easily emphasize the internal adequacy of any symbol the dream might draft to do its emotional work. All that may be needed is a blank check on which the dream can write the emotional sum it wants to expend. This is possible because in the dream state the emotion precedes the image, calls it into being. In this sense we might compare the dream to the rough draft of a

[33]Wilhelm Stekel, *The Interpretation of Dreams: New Developments and Technique,* trans. Eden and Cedar Paul (New York: Washington Square Press, 1967), p. 5.

fiction. Anyone who has tried to write knows the frustration of reaching an impasse in the story. "What I need here," he might say, "is an event that will motivate my hero's departure from Cleveland." As yet, the event is not clear in the mind, but the emotional force needed to move the story forward is quite clearly *felt*. So we have a narrative gap filled by pure or as-yet-ungrounded emotion. But even though the writer has not found the event, he can write an "X" in his plot, or supply a weak substitute that will serve temporarily. In this sense, we may say that the story is emotionally perfect though artistically unrealized. And it is exactly in this sense that we are all Shakespeares when we dream. In certain complex cases at least, all that is minimally necessary for the flow of the dream is that it find images that can be endowed with emotion. Thus, while dreaming, say, in the key of terror, or having established an atmosphere of impending terror, I might be terrified by the sudden appearance of a caged parrot I had seen that afternoon in a pet shop. This parrot is not necessarily a terrifying symbol of, say, imprisonment, though the cage may have served in a minor way to trip the terror switch; it may simply be a tentative analogue that is conscripted and bathed in terror. By fictional standards it is hardly a successful character, but it is a bird in the hand. And given the amazing speed at which the dream unfolds, how, as Burke would say, could it be expected on the spot to come up with the perfect carrier of the emotion of terror—especially if this parrot from the day-residue had complicated things further by hopping about in the environs of the dream?

I have been using the word "symbol" in a loose and possibly confusing sense, and it is time to examine the whole concept of *dream symbolism*. This is the most deeply ingrained principle of Freud's legacy to psychoanalysis, and it is reenforced by the fact that the technique of sym-

bolic interpretation works so well on so many other projects—for instance, literary texts and visual art. But the
goal and delight of symbolism in poetry and art is that it be
recognized as such; even if some symbols are difficult or
esoteric, we somehow know they are symbols. By "symbol," of course, we are referring to anything that seems to
be bearing more than its own semantic weight. In the
sentence "I must mow the grass today," grass is probably
not a symbol (that would depend on the context) because
it arouses no connotations. But in Carl Sandburg's "I am
the grass: let me work," it is clear that grass is something
more than a tonsorial nuisance. In other words, the making of a symbol, unless it is given as such in advance (the
cross, the lion, etc.), involves a kind of semantic de-
familiarization in which the image hides as much as it
reveals. If a word goes past you with a complicitous look
about it, it is probably a symbol.

For Freud, however, all or most symbols strive to be of
the "I must mow the grass today" variety; their purpose is
to slip latent dream-thoughts into the dream in disguised
form.[34] When the dream has a choice, Freud says, it will
select a symbol that will blend denotatively into the environment of the dream so as not to be seen, thereby
suppressing further whatever obvious symbolism it may
have carried in advance. For example, in one dream Freud
tells us that what was probably a bundle of asparagus ("No
knowledgeable person of either sex will ask for an interpretation of asparagus")[35] was disguised in the color of
black radishes, making it unrecognizable to the skeptical
woman shopper who refused to buy it. In another instance,
Freud cites the incomplete research of K. Schrötter who
suggested dream topics to patients under deep hypnosis.

[34]Freud, *SE* 5:352.
[35]Freud, *SE* 4:184.

Freud writes: "If he [Schrötter] gave a suggestion that the subject should dream of normal or abnormal sexual intercourse, the dream, in obeying the suggestion, would make use of symbols familiar to us from psycho-analysis in place of the sexual material."[36] In one such dream, when a female subject was given the suggestion that she dream of having homosexual intercourse with a friend, the friend appeared in the dream carrying a "shabby hand-bag with the label stuck on it bearing the words 'Ladies only'" (p. 384). Because Schrötter's work exists only in sketchy form, Freud does not make much of the point, but it offers a convenient means of approaching the issue of sexual symbolism in dreams. The imagery in the dream above certainly seems sexual, though this does not really define the function of the imagery. We do not know what kinds of controls Schrötter's experiments involved, but standard scientific method would indicate that he made both nonsexual and sexual suggestions to his hypnotized subjects. Suppose, for example, he had suggested that his subject dream of having a pleasant picnic with friends. Presumably (if the suggestion worked) the woman would not dream literally of a picnic, any more than she dreamed literally of homosexual intercourse.[37] More likely, the dream would take the form of a symbolic picnic in which picniclike materials might appear in a nonpicnic setting. Suppose, for example, the woman dreamed she was carrying a basket and eating a pickle, a sausage, or even an asparagus spear while visiting a sick friend in the city. Would this be a clear indication that the suggestion had taken and that the woman was substitut-

---

[36]Freud, *SE* 5:384.

[37]As an example of the manner in which dreamers react vaguely to hypnotic suggestion, see Theodore X. Barber, P. C. Walker, and K. W. Hahn, "Effects of Hypnotic Induction and Suggestions on Nocturnal Dreaming and Thinking," *Journal of Abnormal Psychology* 82 (1973):414–427.

ing picnic symbols for the real thing? If so, it is an "innocent" dream, which Freud would not allow. But now the
case is complicated by symbols that normally have strong
sexual connotations in psychoanalysis. In fact, when one
thinks about it, almost everything one takes on a picnic has
a sexual shape (bowls, cups, knives, spoons, etc.). Is it
possible that we are dealing here with only a *manifest* picnic
dream, one in which the latent content is really sexual
(eating itself suggesting body indulgence), even though the
hypnotist had clearly ordered a picnic dream? Can symbols
be sexual on one occasion and innocently recreational on
another? If so, how can one know that they are repressive
sexual symbols in one case and openly expressive of almost
anything else in the other? What would be the point of a
"repressed" picnic dream—unless it were the dream of the
nude lady in Manet's *Le Déjeuner sur l'herbe?*

In effect, then, Freud asks us to believe that the mind
creates symbols whose symbolic value—even the awareness that they are symbols—is lost on the dreamer. This is
another of Wittgenstein's complaints about Freud's method: "Consider the difficulty that if a symbol in a dream is
not understood, it does not seem to be a symbol at all. So
why call it one?"[38] Freud, he said, was really thinking
about symbolism from the perspective of the analyst and
what the dreamer could be brought to accept. In this connection, he notes (as have many others) that Freud does
not deal with explicitly sexual dreams. The obvious implication is that in such dreams the theory of symbolism
and disguise would be at its most vulnerable, for what
could be the subtext of a sexual dream? Moreover, on the
grounds of Freud's belief that there is always an opposition
between the latent and the manifest contents, an openly
sexual dream would lead to the apparent absurdity that it

[38]Wittgenstein, *Lectures and Conversations,* p. 44.

was masking a nonsexual content. In any case, it seems highly improbable that a dream would openly produce images of sexual organs one night and disguise them the next night as turnips, black radishes, top hats, or open doorways unless there were something other than censorship at stake—that is, a true symbolic expressiveness such as that aimed for by the artist, though for altogether different purposes. I must immediately add that by expressiveness, once again, I do not imply that the dream is expressing anything for the dreamer's immediate benefit or understanding. It is not a linguistic expressiveness but one devoted to the classification of experience. In making my analogy between art and dreaming, then, I am thinking of art not as the familiar instrument of our pleasure and instruction, but as a process by which the brain determines what goes with what in human experience. In art, as in dreams, we process the patterns and qualities of life, never its precise content—memory being less like a computer than it is like metaphor, that is, a kind of orderly mistake.

2 *Involuntary Poetry*

L ET US return to the idea that the brain uses sleep time to sort out and integrate experience and that as one of its main operations this process involves the superimposition of new experience on experience that has already been stored. The dream-work would seem to resemble a librarian adding new books to a shelf and pausing to browse among the books already there. It even appears that the brain has an intricate cross-reference system, meaning, as Francis Crick and Graeme Mitchison put it, that one synapse is capable of storing several distinct pieces of information and that "a particular piece of information [may be] distributed over very many synapses."[1] For example, we all have a category of *fears* in which very dissimilar things are stored in terms of an emotion they arouse. If you ask me to name things I fear, my "fears" category immediately disgorges its data: snakes, insects (hairy), high places, caves, and all small enclosures, deep water, and so on, back through fears I have all but forgotten—like darkness and Fred Potts, the bully who tormented me in grade

[1]Francis Crick and Graeme Mitchison, "The Function of Dream Sleep," *Nature*, July 14, 1983, p. 111.

school. It is an astounding feat, this ability to muster such unlike things under a single common denominator on an instant's notice. And it is even more complex, for while I can say that Fred Potts in a certain way reminds me of a snake or an insect, I cannot very well say that he reminds me of a high place, although by another categorical operation it is possible that I may encounter him one night while I am dizzily clinging to a ledge on a deep canyon wall. It is even possible, by still another maneuver, that my brain will run its Potts program backward and he will be the instrument of my rescue. And so it proceeds through an infinity of call numbers in the neural library, which, scientists assure us, has a virtually infinite capacity for storage and combination.

One of my assumptions is that we have only one brain and that the operations of the dream must therefore have a considerable kinship to those of conscious thought. To put it more immediately, as image makers the poet and the dreamer go to the same well, or at least use the same bucket. But we should also draw a distinction between dream-thought and conscious thought of all kinds. It is generally agreed that the province of dream-thought is the visual image. Whether or how we actually *see* the dream image is a neurological technicality. If nothing else, we invoke the metaphor of the mind's eye because all the characteristics of the dream image are visual. Even the eyes of the body, as REM indicates, seem to be seeing the dream as it occurs in the brain—a physiological absurdity, of sorts. Words play a secondary role in the dream; smells, sounds, and touch play even smaller roles. On the other hand, the province of waking-thought is something like language—not precisely or always language, of course, but something that relies heavily on the linearity of word-structures, logical relations, and so on. And there is every reason to assume that there is a level of prelinguistic

thought analogous to that of preimagistic thought. This is
the realm of mental activity that Nelson Goodman refers
to as "unuttered utterances" and "invisible pictures,"[2] and
at bottom they may be one and the same thing.

Actually, I am using some distinctions Frederic Bartlett
makes in one of the more durable and readable studies of
brain activity. Words, he says, "differ from images [in
that] they can indicate the qualitative and relational features of a situation in their *general* aspect just as directly as,
and perhaps more satisfactorily than, they can describe its
peculiar individuality." Words "succeed just where . . .
images tend most conspicuously to break down: they can
name the general as well as describe the particular, and
since they deal in formulated connexions they more
openly bear their logic with them."[3] In all mental exer-
tions, thinking and image-making cooperate, somewhat
like dialectic and myth in Socratic thought, where the
mythical is "the immediate temporality and spaciality" of
the Idea.[4] Thus, in practice, image and thought combine,
as Bartlett says. Each takes over some of the peculiarities
of the other, so that "images . . . seem to be striving after
some general significance and framework, while language
often builds its links from case to case upon elaborate and
detailed individual description" (p. 226). Put simply, the
province of the image is analogy and association, of unit-
ing "realms of interest not conventionally put together"

[2]Nelson Goodman, "On Thoughts without Words," *Cognition* 12
(1982): 212–213; reprinted in Nelson Goodman, *Of Mind and Other
Matters* (Cambridge, Mass.: Harvard University Press, 1984), pp. 22–
23.

[3]Frederic C. Bartlett, *Remembering: A Study in Experimental and Social
Psychology* (Cambridge: Cambridge University Press, 1932), p. 225.

[4]See Søren Kierkegaard, *The Concept of Irony, with Constant Reference
to Socrates,* trans. Lee M. Capel (Bloomington: Indiana University
Press, 1965), p. 132.

(p. 223); the province of word-thinking is meaning, significance, maintaining connections that have been established by prior thought. Thus the image, in its intimate cooperation with thought, is the means by which "a man can take out of its setting something that happened a year ago, reinstate it with much if not all of its individuality unimpaired, combine it with something that happened yesterday, and use them both to help him solve a problem with which he is confronted today" (p. 219). And if we reverse Bartlett's order, so it is with the dream. By means of the image, the brain can take out of its setting something that happened today, combine it with something that happened in the near or distant past, and use the resultant composite image as a figure in the expression of a feeling common to both temporal zones. Or it can file today's experience, thus amended, thus scrambled, in the storehouse of past experience, where it becomes not simply a part of a history but a tool for the acquisition of the future. Memory, Gerald Edelman says, "is not a replicative recall of stored physical descriptors. It is an imaginative act, a form of dynamic recategorization. . . . Its very lack of repetitive precision . . . is the source of creative possibility for generalization and pattern recognition."[5] Freud's idea "that every dream [is] linked in its manifest content with recent experiences and in its latent content with the most ancient experiences"[6] would be perfectly consistent with Edelman's "Darwinian" theory of memory. One content, however, is not a censorship of the other; instead it is metaphorically joined to or correlated with the other. The recent experience finds its equivalent in the material of memory. Like a homing pigeon it finds

[5]Gerald M. Edelman, "Neural Darwinism: Population Thinking and Higher Brain Function," in *How We Know*, ed. Michael Shafto (San Francisco: Harper & Row, 1985), p. 24.
[6]Freud, *SE* 4:218.

its way back to its emotional roost. From this point of view, we might describe the dream as our unwitting "interception," in Evans' term, of the filing of experience into categories of resemblance; what seems to occur, imagistically, as a single experience (the dream plot) is really a combination of experiences that share common characteristics.

To sum up, during the day our life is dominated by language, or by the verbal and sequential facility, the need to communicate, and therefore by conventional behavior and meaning. We are, as Bartlett says, "caught up in generalities" (p. 226). The day, relatively speaking, is the enemy of the idiosyncratic, of the unique personal life that can thrive only when we are alone. But at night, when language (as such) declines, the image faculty arises in almost pure unattended form to organize the interests kept apart not only by the day but also by the sequence of all our days. Thus Macbeth's line "Sleep that knits up the ravell'd sleave of care" has a literal and biological truth. For the metaphor of sleep and its handmaiden the dream, stitching up our raveled day experiences in an attempt to make them into a fabric—in effect, a slightly new fabric in which "all our yesterdays" are slightly amended by today—offers a new possibility with respect to the function and the mechanism of the dream. It may be that the specific content of the dream's "cares" is less important than the brain's need to knit the cares, whatever they may be, and to allow the image mechanism to sharpen the needles by which it makes a fabric of life rather than a haphazard history of sequences.

If we can assume that dreaming is our most conscious manifestation of this process of storage and integration, then we have good cause to reexamine the whole notion of dream symbolism. The use of the term "symbol" probably originates in the strangeness of many dream images and in the unreal or imaginary nature of all dreams. Our natural response to the dream is "What does it *mean?*" But if we shift our ground from meaning to classification, and thence to expressiveness, the term "symbol," in its psychoanalytic meaning, becomes almost irrelevant, for we now have a means of explaining the seeming strangeness of dream images that has nothing to do with substitution and concealment. In effect, we reach the basis of the similarity between dreams and art as ways of "cataloging" experience through common mental procedures.

The most eloquent case for an aesthetics of dreaming is made by the philosopher Gaston Bachelard. Here is a key passage from his *Earth and the Reveries of the Will:*

> But if we limit ourselves, as psychoanalysis often does, to translating symbols into human terms, we neglect an entire field of study—the autonomy of symbolism. . . . It is true that psychoanalysis evaluates dominant impulses by their results. But it has not prepared the means for a true *psychical dynamics,* a precise dynamics investigating the individuality of images. In other words, psychoanalysis merely defines images by their symbolism. As soon as an instinctual image has been detected or a traumatic memory brought to light, psychoanalysis raises the question of *social* interpretation. It neglects an entire domain of research: the very domain of the imagination, whereas the psyche is animated by a veritable *hunger for images.* It wants images. In sum, under the image, psychoanalysis seeks reality; it ignores the inverse investigation that starts from reality in order to seek the positive character of the image. It is in this research that we detect that imaginative energy that is the very mark of the active psyche.[7]

[7]Gaston Bachelard, *On Poetic Imagination and Reverie,* trans. Colette Gaudin (New York: Bobbs-Merrill, 1971), p. 67. The passage appears in *La Terre et les rêveries de la volonté* (Paris: Librairie José Corti, 1948), pp. 19–20.

Bachelard is more concerned with reverie than with the nocturnal dream (which, he says in *The Poetics of Reverie,* "does not belong to us. It is not our possession"), but for my purposes the difference in focus is negligible. Thus, for Bachelard, the ubiquitous reverie (or dream) of flight, which psychoanalysts typically interpret as a symbol of sensual desire, becomes an expression of "the aesthetics of gracefulness": "Dynamic imagination suggests, to one who contemplates a graceful line, the wildest substitution: it is you, dreamer, who are the evolving grace. Feel in yourself the *force of gracefulness*. Realize that you are a reserve of gracefulness, a potentiality of flight. Understand that you hold, within your very will, curled volutes, like the young tender fern."[8] As dream interpretation, this would scarcely pass on the analytic couch. But Bachelard is not really interpreting this dream, and certainly not substituting one symbolism (grace) for another (desire). The dream of flight is here not a symbol at all, but an "emulation," a "transcendence of being," wherein the dream, in symbiotic conspiracy with the sleeping body, acts out an impossibility, "gives sustenance to our instinct of verticality." The dream of flight is, in an un-Freudian sense, a wish fulfillment that could not be improved by the possession of real wings.

Let us consider Bachelard's idea that the psyche is animated by a hunger for images. As an explanation of the dream-mechanism, this is an extremely poetic notion, but it is one I want to press here, if only to see where it might lead. For the present, let us confine our interest to the hunger itself and ignore the nature of the images it produces. Perhaps the best way to coax the notion out of its

[8]Bachelard, *On Poetic Imagination,* pp. 65–66. From *L'Air et les songes: Essai sur l'imagination du mouvement* (Paris: Librairie José Corti, 1943), pp. 28–29.

metaphorical cloak is to recast it in more phenomenological terms. In Sartre's essay on the dream in *The Psychology of Imagination*, we have a thesis that overlaps Bachelard's. Sartre spends more than two hundred pages defining the nature of the image and the consciousness that produces it. At the risk of oversimplification, I reduce the relevant part of his thesis to something like this: In the dream, consciousness cannot *perceive*, or reflect, because it is "imprisoned" in the imaginative attitude. What characterizes this attitude is that "it has lost the very idea of reality" and therefore lacks the power to compare the dream with a reality that might perform the "function of a reducer," or corrective.[9] Thus, if the consciousness, in the hypnagogic interval before sleep, somehow conceives a dot of entoptic light as a fish, it may become "persuaded" that the fish "has a story" and go on, in a dream, to put the fish into a lake, bring on a fisherman, and have the fish end up on the archbishop's table. What has happened here is that consciousness has been completely "taken in." It enters completely "into the game and it itself [is] determined to produce syntheses in all their richness, but only in an imaginary way." In short, consciousness is "carried along by its own decline and it continues to lay hold of images indefinitely." This, Sartre says, "is the real explanation of oniric [*sic*] symbolism:"

> If consciousness can never take hold of its own anxieties, its own desires, excepting as symbols, it is not, as Freud believed, because of a suppression which compels it to disguise them: but because it is incapable of laying hold of what there is of the real under its form of reality. It has completely lost the function of the real and everything it feels, everything it thinks, it cannot feel or think otherwise

[9]Jean Paul Sartre, *The Psychology of Imagination*, trans. Bernard Frechtman (New York: Washington Square Press, 1968), p. 214.

than under the imagined form. . . . This is the reason why the world of the dream like that of the reader occurs as completely magical; we are haunted by the adventures of the persons of our dream as we are by the heroes of a novel. . . . This is what gives the dream its unique nuance of fatality. The events occur as if not being able not to happen, in correlation with a consciousness which cannot help imagining them (pp. 218–220).

In some respects we are beyond Bachelard here, and there is probably a sense in which Sartre's helpless consciousness is not the same thing as Bachelard's hungry psyche. (For one thing, Sartre is not much concerned with the poetics of dreaming.) But in either case we arrive at much the same thing: a consciousness that, cut off from all recourse to "the category of the real," is forced to feed on its own imaginative productions. Consciousness is like a child "imprisoned" in a playpen with only a set of blocks. If it is to obey its body's impulse to grow and to mature, it has no choice but to realize the possibilities of these instruments of creation, to "produce syntheses in all their richness." Image follows image, not because the mind thinks up the images (as a novelist thinks up "next" events), but because the world of the dream, unfolding in the world of the body, is one of perpetual motion in which figures are constantly and rapidly transformed, taking the path of least resistance—or better, the path of greatest suggestibility. To give one of Sartre's examples, if the dreamer is in danger he does not say "I wish I had a revolver"—he suddenly *has* one. "But too bad for him if at that very moment a thought should occur to him which in the waking world would assume the form of 'What if the revolver had been locked!' This 'if' cannot exist in the dream: this rescuing revolver is suddenly locked at the very moment when it is needed" (p. 221).

66

We must try to see more clearly what kind of force has produced this radical transformation in the revolver—that is, what exactly is behind these concepts of "hunger" and "fatalism," or what I have called the path of greatest suggestibility. Let us take a dream situation most of us know well. It begins with the appearance in the dream community of a terrible monster. Everyone is fleeing, and the dream shows scenes in which people are being trampled and eaten. You, the dreamer, try to escape, but your limbs are suddenly sluggish, uncooperative. You manage to hide but the tree or rock is too small to conceal you—*or* the monster *knows* where you are. You are trapped. If the dream is terrifying enough, you may awake abruptly, but there is an equal chance that you will be seized and eaten, all the while regarding your dismemberment with great concern but little pain.

There are two ways of looking at such a dream. Freud says that every dream is "absolutely egotistical," that it treats of oneself exclusively. In short, if there is a monster at large, you are its Dr. Frankenstein. The monster has been created in the laboratory of your nonsensory thought to the specifications of your own fear (like Winston's rats in the novel *1984*). But we may look at the dream another way. Under the flesh of this private monster is the skeletal form of all monsters. What I have in mind here is not a Jungian archetype but what we may for convenience call "the law of the locked revolver." It is the law that may turn a pleasant dream-reunion with one's father into a nightmare of rejection. On a more delicate level of operation, it is the law that may convert a slight change in facial expression to a complete change of personality or, to return to an earlier example, that may allow my mother suddenly to assume the face and body of a complete stranger. All these radical changes—and all dream changes are not radical—are brought about by *the drive* of consciousness, its unreflecting seizure of a nuance in the dream image or situation and the conversion of this nuance to something else. A question now arises: How is this seizure-conversion process controlled by the dream-work? How does the dream know enough to invent a plot rather than a chaotic sequence of images? It is evident that some instinct for storytelling survives the decline of consciousness into the dream state and allows the image to "radiate," in Bachelard's word, in an *expressive direction*. Here we are verging on the true artistic character of the dream, the sense in which it follows, however inefficiently, the same instinct that animates fictions, especially the highly dramatic fiction (i.e., the monster dream). Moreover, in the dream state the very loss of "the category of the real," with all its strictures and demands, opens consciousness to more radical resources of metaphor and imagery than those permitted the poet; these resources are no different in kind from those of poetry, but only immensely more personal. In any event, the dream should be compared not to a completed work of fiction or cinema but to the process of composition itself—that is, it creates as it goes. We can scarcely say that this has anything to do with "quality control" or with the kinds of coherence that writers strive to achieve *as they write*. It strikes me instead as being a matter of the dreamer inadvertently composing the dream as it occurs—for example, in thinking "The path is going to give way" or "The car is going to crash" the dreamer assures that the content of the next event is being prepared. Similarly, the novelist prepares his next events out of what we might call vectorial prediction, whereby anticipation is converted into occurrence. It is not this simple, because dreams are filled with unexpected happenings, but the dire quality of some dreams must arise from this principle of catastrophic expectancy. We might also account for the development of dream plots by the analogy of improvisational acting. The basis of this training technique usually is to allow two or more actors to interact spontaneously with each other, sometimes in a certain emotional "key"—hostility, friendliness, suspicion, and so forth. One actor in, say, a situation of hostility will make a hostile gesture or movement, and another actor will respond in kind. The point is that the next development in the scene will arise from the previous gesture, it will be a reactive continuation of it. Nothing will have been planned in advance, yet a narrative that has some coherence does get acted, at least within a series of adjacent units. And this seems to be the case with dreams. The narrative coherence is rather brief (places shift, people come and go, etc.), though the overall mood of the dream may remain.

So, however different, the imperatives that may motivate the dream and poetic art spring from the same creatural "talent" that precedes poetic skill and manifests itself in some form on all levels of thought. Among other things, it is an instinct for thoroughness (or what I will later discuss under the tropological category of "irony"). "Where," Bachelard writes, "is the fear which does not become exaggerated?" Or, we may add, where is the pleasure, the desire, or the grief? This exaggeration of all concerns, in waking life as in dream life, is the natural inclination of the imagination to envision "the worst of all worst worsts" or, as in happy dreams, the best of all best bests. Thus the dream, though not all dreams, outrageously obeys the dialectical impulse, the unuttered "What if?" that regulates all normal life.

Of course, we are looking at the dream from a constructional rather than clinical perspective. The difference can be quickly illustrated by citing the well-known cartoon (used by Freud and Rank) of the dream of the French nurse. Here we move in eight panels from a child urinating on the sidewalk to the formation of a stream, then a river, and finally an ocean on which increasingly larger boats are navigating the child's unstoppable flow. In the last panel the nurse awakens with the appearance of an ocean liner to find the wet child crying in bed. Freud sees the cartoon as the paradigm of the dream as the guardian of sleep: "The ingenious artist has in this way cleverly depicted the struggle between an obstinate craving for sleep and an inexhaustible stimulus towards waking."[10] While this may be true, the cartoon also explains how dream images behave *thoroughly,* with or without the external stimulus or the craving for sleep. Here we have a perfect illustration of the conversion of a dream image along the path of greatest suggestibility. Once the dream commits itself to an abundant flow of water, it seizes the obvious associations until it exhausts the potential or reaches a point where something else commands its interest. Here we arrive at the infralevels of dream organization, where the dream probably behaves according to personal and idiosyncratic rules that are impossible to follow. In any case, I want to amend Freud's eogtistical theory of the dream to include at least one law of formal progression: Dr. Frankenstein (the dreamer) indeed creates his own monster along self-ish lines, but once animated, made real, by his "science," it becomes the creature of a fiction, it inherits a destiny—to be the best, most monstrous monster possible, to cooperate (like Judas, Iago, and the white whale) in the drama of Frankenstein's undoing. Thus in our dreams, as in our fictions, we find ourselves, as hero-creator, coaxed to the verge of possibility: imagination demands nothing less than our own head on the block, our own body (or the body of a loved one) in the path of the monster, the bullet, and the spear. It does not follow that the dream is the impersonal creation of fictional rules. When the image, say, of a hostile father recurs in an individual's dreams, it

[10]Freud, *SE* 5:367.

points to an alarming problem, and this is why psychia-
trists are right to place so much emphasis on the dream
series. But in a single "normal" dream, a hostile father is
simply a highly personalized variation of the monster principle. It means nothing more than that the dreamer's imagination has made thorough use of a fear that has crossed
every son's or daughter's mind.

Not all dreams, perhaps not even most dreams, are
marked by such dialectical thoroughness as my monster
dream. I have simply tried to illustrate an extreme that
would probably qualify as a nightmare. and before con-
cluding this preparation for my more detailed treatment of
"the rhetoric of dreams" I would like to sample expressiveness in a less violent form. What goes on in a
dream, I have suggested, is not an act of censorship or
disguise, but a transformation of feelings, emotions, or
thoughts into their imagistic equivalents. Suppose a dream
wanted to express the act of cutting a diamond, but also
wanted to recover the delicacy and tact of such a operation. Could the unlikely tool to be used for this purpose
not be a flower petal or a feather? And in such a case, need
the interpreter chase about among the various sexual sym-
bolisms of flowers in order to account for this radical
"censorship" of the diamond cutter's proper equipment?
In short, should we not allow the creative possibility that
dream artistry might employ anything as a metaphor for
its preoccupation as long as it caught the quality of the
experience? If we think of the image as standing in an
adjectival relationship to the noun or feeling to be expressed, *which the dream already knows,* we might fully account for the peculiar aura of vividness that attends many
dreams. However, let me take a dangerously sexual case,
one that might stand as a paradigm of dream censorship.
Here, in effect, is a specimen dream that will demonstrate
what I mean by expressiveness. It is the by now rather

famous dream of a twenty-four-year-old college student, and it comes from the dream collection of Calvin Hall, who is so taken by its charms that he mentions it frequently in his work on "normal" dreams:

> I got out of bed and went into the bathroom and attempted to turn on the water faucet. I turned and turned but no water came out. I then decided to call a plumber. Soon afterwards the door opened and an individual dressed in coveralls approached me. Upon closer examination I discovered the plumber was a female. I scoffed at the idea of a lady plumber, but unruffled she went to the basin, turned the faucet, and water immediately flowed. An emission occurred.[11]

Hall is that rare psychologist who is keenly appreciative of the creative aspect of dreaming. He is strenuously opposed to the Freudian idea that the dream image is a disguise behind which repressed materials are smuggled into the dream. "The symbols of dreams," he says, "are there to express something, not to hide it,"[12] and in illustration he cites another dream in which this same young man, finding himself in another sexual situation, has no trouble calling a spade a spade: "I tried to seduce her only to discover that my organ seemed too large for her vagina, thus making intercourse impossible."[13] In other words, it is just as likely that a dream will be outspoken as it is that it will hide behind a symbol. And the question then occurs: "Why did the dreamer choose to represent his sex organ by a faucet?" Hall gives several answers. "The choice of faucet expressed [his] conception of his penis on the night

[11]Calvin S. Hall, "Out of a Dream Came the Faucet," *Psychoanalysis and the Psychoanalytic Review* 49 (Winter 1962): 113.

[12]Calvin S. Hall, *The Meaning of Dreams* (New York: McGraw-Hill, 1966), p. 95.

[13]Hall, "Out of a Dream," p. 114.

of February 22, 1948"; he was "dissatisfied with the referent object and creat[ed] a better one. Our young dreamer thought to himself, 'wouldn't it be nice if my penis could be turned on and off as easily as a faucet.' No sooner thought than visualized" (p. 114). And in still another article Hall adds that this faucet represents a "purely mechanical conception of sex."[14]

However outrageous it may seem, we can go beyond these explanations if we apply the techniques of literary criticism to the dream—in other words, if we try to view this dream as the product of creative logic rather than the personal whimsy of the dreamer. To begin, the dream bristles with questions relating to the whole mystery of dreaming and the extraordinary use dreams make of the principles of anticipation, development, reversal, and (I can't avoid a pun here) climax. There is nothing extraneous in it, at least as reported, and even if embellished in the telling it is faithful in spirit to dreams we have all had. It is true that most dreams are not this well organized; indeed, we have here an unusually succinct summing up of what must (as I hope to show) have been a complex situation.

What is lacking in the dream is the aura of fantasy. It is a "realistic" dream with none of the surreal images that often intrude in dreams. It could have actually happened— a young man could have been sexually aroused, also could have had a frozen bathroom faucet, and could have called a plumber who turned out to be the perfect (if unexpected) answer to both his problems. But this is not the case, and we are faced with the questions: Why did he imagine his penis as a faucet? Why was he so "dissatisfied," on this particular night, with his "referent object"?

---

[14]Calvin S. Hall, "A Cognitive Theory of Dreams," *Journal of General Psychology* 49 (1953): 277.

Here indeed is a polemical dream, an example of "useful" art. But the small miracle is that it did not accomplish its purpose (ejaculation) simply by producing an image (like the rabbit) which could be endowed with sexual energy. Instead, the dream produced a plot, a chain of events that *led* to ejaculation, though nowhere in this plot do we find anything (an unclothed woman, a sexual pass) that has an openly sexual character (as in the young man's other dream). Why should the dream be so roundabout—so "Jamesian," one might say—when that is clearly not necessary to produce an emission? If the dreamer simply wanted a symbol that would represent a mechanical conception of sex, it would have been easy to invent a faucet or a faucetlike penis, without the elaborate subterfuge of a lady plumber. In other words, if the dream is simply symbolizing in order to express the mechanical quality of sex, or even if it is repressing open sexuality, there is a considerable amount of excess artwork in the dream, and this leads one to believe that the art was necessary for the expression of an experience far richer than one that would interest a clinician, if only because the richness is subdiagnostic.

I suggest that the faucet *is* a disguise, but not in the sense of a repression. It is a disguise that was necessary for the internal success of the dream situation. Here we have an image of a high order of expressiveness. The faucet is a symbol not only of the male organ (in this case, an absent noun) but also of a particular social situation that has nothing to do with sex. In fact, we have a dream situation very like Burke's case of the dream that is interrupted by the dreamer's sudden urge to urinate. The difference is that the faucet dream manages to steer brilliantly between its high and low motives by producing an image that is literally a double-agent. We might describe the dream situation as follows: The precise nuance of sexual encounter that was on the dreamer's mind that night clearly involved the need for sexual release, rather than, for example, the titillation of seduction or the pleasure or frustration of the sexual act itself. As we say, there is sex, and then there is sex. In any case, the means of release is absent as the dream begins, and it must be imported into the dream. Dealing with these two "facts," the dream was compelled, on the one hand, to invent an excuse to bring a partner to the room and, on the other hand, to find a penis symbol that would suggest flow (as opposed to tumescence, sensitivity, or any other characteristic of sex or the sex organ). In the face of this demanding problem, the faucet was an excellent compromise because it so realistically displaced the dream's sexual objective into a normal social channel. Knowing nothing else about the young man's private life or his possible sex neurosis, I am suggesting that this particular dream called for the observation of a certain protocol. The euphemistic premise of the dream is that it reach its nefarious end by keeping things aboveboard, by deviating the woman's sexual function to the realm of household repair. Seen in this light, there is just enough fetishistic subtlety in the faucet device to bring on an orgasm through the very perfection of the disguise. Skillfully, the dream harnesses the world of public service to the private needs of the body without so much as a whisper about sex. In fact, we might locate the fictional perfection of this tactic in those downright sexy scenes in the work of Henry James, the master of erotic symbolism, that take place over high tea or in the manicured gardens of London and Europe. Finally, what a rich detail the scoffing is, considered as a conspiracy of dream and dreamer. Here is a stroke of casuistry designed to keep the sexual encounter where the dream has pitched it. "Unruffled" indeed, the woman turns on the faucet (which was, after all, in good working order) and leaves (can we see a certain *hauteur* in her departure?), the unsuspecting victim of a male fantasy acted out without risk of embarrassment or loss of face.

This is of course a literary interpretation of the dream's motive, and I hope the reader will have gathered that I do not exactly mean all I have said in such an aggressive "close reading" of this slight text. I do not mean that dreams are this clever in finessing their plots or that this or any dream is as "good" as the most mediocre fiction. The idea is that what looks from the diagnostic standpoint like substitution and censorship can be seen from another standpoint as a delicate pursuit of emotional equivalence. Some sexual dreams must find their equivalences in non-sexual realms of imagery, and, as I hope to illustrate later, some nonsexual dreams can best express their experience in sexual terms. No procedure is barred from the dream, and all images have the same status in the dream-work. With the exception perhaps of dreams of very disturbed people, the relationship between the manifest and latent contents of a dream is nothing more than the relationship between a modifier and its subject. The subject is always a feeling in search of an image; it is absent from the dream, but it is what holds the dream together. To "read" the dream without knowing the feeling—which I have had to with the young man's dream—is somewhat like reading the auguries of bird intestines or tea leaves.

It may have been unfair to select an unusually complete dream as my illustration of expressiveness, but I simply wanted to approximate a certain integrity common to dreams though not so available in most dream plots. For example, it would be difficult to discuss that far more pervasive kind of dream "genius" that arises when we create a wholly real character out of fragments of remembered life, or when we place an acquaintance in a situation perfectly expressive of his speech and manner. We write a chapter of his life that he will never live, yet he lives it to the hilt, *in character*—so much so that on the next meeting we can only regard him with a thief's sense of guilt, or relish.

My larger point is not that psychiatry is wrong about the dream, but that it is simply half right. There is an imaginative overlay in dreams that is no more explained by psychoanalysis than Kafka's novels are explained by his obsession with paternal authority. There is nothing mysterious about this. It is a talent we all possess. But it is less related to that rare ability to create fine art in waking life than to the natural recognition with which we receive the art of poets and painters and know, though we could not say why, where it succeeds and where it falters and tells lies about life.

It is not a question of the dream following poetic rules, but something more like the reverse. Jean Paul Richter, from whom I take my chapter title, says that dreaming is involuntary poetry, but one could as well put the case that poetry is voluntary dreaming. The point is that poetry is intended for an audience of "others" and must therefore follow certain rules; it must make a certain sense, have a certain unity of impression, and so on. The poetic image introduces us to something that is somehow *right* because we know it from experience: beauty *can* be cold, kindness *can* be cruel, and dawns *do* walk over the eastward hill. But the dream image presents rightness from the remove of an *inner* logic. Even the waking dreamer is perplexed by the image he has made, for the image was forged with an utter disregard for what belongs with what in the waking world. But the originality of the dream can be astonishing. How could my body possibly think up such a unique and stupendous castle from its storehouse of castles remembered from stories, paintings, motion pictures, and tours through real castles? How was my brain capable of making *that* last night when today I cannot even conjure a clear image of my cat? Through what neural agency of the imagination can I dream a sublime landscape that outdoes the landscapes of Turner and Wordsworth? Or am I as deluded about the quality of my dreamscapes as I was about the quality of last night's dream-poetry or the revolutionary philosophical theory I carried to the academy in a wheelbarrow? I am defending the miracle of how dream images come into being, not their artistic quality. The fact is, dreams are artless. They are not "made" to serve as art, and they cannot be regarded by the dreamer with the aesthetic distance from which we regard art, which is strictly a category of reality. In dreams the "willing suspension of disbelief" is replaced by a suspension of discrimination respecting the real and the imaginary. (Hence a banging shutter has the same ontological status as the pistol shot that pierces the dreamer's chest.) The true common denominator of art-making and dreaming is the production of images, and it is more accurate to say that art is like dreaming than that dreaming is like art. The dream precedes art both in the history of the race and in the history of the individual psyche. If we conceive the province of imagery as the province of association, transition, and essence (the *quality* of anything), as against the province of grammar and analysis—which is that of logic, order, and development (beginning-and-endness)—we may see the dream as the nearest thing to what we might call pure imagery, or imagery unfettered by plausibility. The dreamer is an image maker with a unique capacity (if we except the madman) to be inside his own images. The dream is an image system with no medium but that of mentation itself, and this is why most analogies of dream and film, or dream and fiction, are substantively false.

Still, the roots of art are in the dream. The image of the poet is the high refinement of the dream's capacity to conceive the impossible. We are so inured by habit and poetic convention that we can scarcely hear the outrageous in the poet's image. "The morn, in russet mantle clad, / Walks o'er the dew of yon high eastward hill" is all but dead from repetition. But if you can untame your eye and *see* it in a certain way, for a split second you are caught in a mini-dream. You could call it uncanny, except that you know it is nothing but art.

PART TWO

THE DREAM WORK

3 *The Tropological Approach*

T HE MOST BAFFLING question about the dream is not
why it distorts its content—if one assumes that it
does—but how it manages to remain so orderly in its
operations. The immense convenience of the concept of an
unconscious is that it assigns the dream-work to a ghostwriter. But having rejected this notion, we must now ask
how it is that, without help from beyond, the dream can
stay on its subject, and in most cases do so far better than
the waking mind in a daydream state. Go for a half-hour
drive or simply stare into space, and chances are your
thoughts will drift from one topic to another and end on
one that has no relation to the first, and in the interval your
mood may have swung ninety degrees, depending on
what your meanderings have unearthed to think or worry
about. In sleep, one would think that a mind free of the
involvements of putting one foot before another and reduced to a helpless receptor of sensation would run away
with itself and produce a chaos of images, or nothing at all.
But this is not the case. In its own terms, the dream is
capable of remarkable control of its materials. In fact, most
dreams are conservative when compared with the distortions we find in poetry and art. We ask that poems be

83

coherent, but to this end they can turn anything into anything else. In a poem "Nimble thought can jump both sea and land," as Shakespeare's Sonnet 44 goes, only because language has no trouble getting from place to place. Therefore, for instance, Macbeth can invent a naked babe striding the apocalyptic blast out of nothing but Duncan's virtue. This makes sense thematically. It is impossible, but poetry does not have to care about that. But it would be an extraordinary dream that offered as much visual fireworks as we get in the space of Macbeth's daydream. We call such things hallucinations, and they are usually the result of a chemically induced alteration in the brain functions. But normal dreams have less radical plots. And they seem to obey a theme—not in the conceptual sense, as we use the term in literature, but in the musical sense of key, or melodic continuity. If the dream is not "logical," it at least dwells on a content; it is an accretion of enigma variations. I am not claiming that all dreams have these characteristics, but many do, and the problem now is to see whether we can make some "waking" sense out of the mental processes that produce dreams.

To think of the dream as something *given* to the dreamer, something made somewhere in him, is to falsify not only the dream but the nature of consciousness as well. We must begin instead with the notion that a dream is the unified act of a synergic system (the body) in which the state we call consciousness is simply the fine-tuning of its self-awareness. The creation of a dream is simultaneous with its appearance. The dream is a phase of being, the organism behaving in one of its ways. For example, dreams do not have beginnings and endings. The significance of this is not that we join the dream in progress, that we see an image when thought has reached a certain pitch, as one hears music when it comes into earshot. This too would imply, however figuratively we speak, that consciousness was in some sense independent of the dream, waiting, so to speak, to *receive* it. The dream, Merleau-Ponty says, is "a direction of our existence":

> When I dream that I am flying or falling, the whole signifi-
> cance of the dream is contained in the flight or the fall, as
> long as I do not reduce them to their physical appearance in
> the waking world, and so long as I take them with all their
> existential implications. The bird which hovers, falls and
> becomes a handful of ash, does not hover and fall in phys-
> ical space; it rises and falls with the existential tide running
> through it, or again it is the pulse of my existence, its
> systole and diastole. . . . In dreaming as in myth we learn
> *where* the phenomenon is to be found, by feeling that to-
> wards which our desire goes out, what our heart dreads, on
> what our life depends.[1]

In other words, I do not *go to* my dream, even metaphorically, as to a film, and it is not a vision that comes to
me. It is the pulse and direction of my existence. I may
have had the dream on Wednesday night and the REM
monitor might determine that it began at 2:14 A.M. and
lasted until 2:26 A.M. But from the phenomenal standpoint
it did not begin. Just as a child cannot possibly detect the
moment at which it became aware of the world, or the
sleeper the moment at which sleep began, the dreamer
cannot detect the beginning of his dream because for that
interval the dream is all of his consciousness that exists.
The dream is the center and the horizon of his world. It is,
like his life, the given out of which consciousness arises,
that was already there, in progress, when he awakened,
within sleep, in the world of the dream—that is, when his
consciousness suddenly condensed itself into a scene.

[1]Maurice Merleau-Ponty, *The Phenomenology of Perception,* trans.
Colin Smith (London: Routledge & Kegan Paul, 1962), p. 285.

I turn now to what I take to be the fundamental executive processes of the dream-work. I see no further reason to speak of symbols (in the Freudian sense) in dreams. There is simply no evidence that dreams speak in a symbolic tongue designed to mask a real meaning. The basic unit of the dream is the image, and because the dream unfolds in the mode of action, it is constantly evolving, never a still picture. Therefore, I shall think of the image as any visual event being elaborated by the dream. But the dream image has a peculiar characteristic. It carries to an extreme a basic condition of perception. We think we see a person or an object as if it were all there before us in plain sight. But we are really seeing it contextually, or perhaps cubistically, if we redefine cubism as being a superimposition of associations on a spatial object. For example, I do not see an arm dangling in the bus aisle in front of me. What I do see is the arm *of a person* who animates it. So perception, as Sartre says, is always contaminated by knowing.[2] But in the dream state, where all objects and people are "chosen" because of associations, the dream world being a continuous reverberation of memory, contamination is an especially strong factor. So much *else* rides on the dream image. As we shall see, this helps account for the extraordinary vividness of many dream images, or the respect in which we "see" much more than is actually there. But it also introduces us to the *incipient* quality of the dream image, or the sense in which, as a mediation between feeling and perception, it is always the vehicle of a transformation, or what we might call a re-semblance. And this brings me to the subject of the tropes.

It has been suggested by several theorists that the principle of metaphor be substituted for that of symbol, but as

[2]Jean-Paul Sartre, *The Psychology of Imagination*, trans. Bernard Frechtman (New York: Washington Square Press, 1968), pp. 118–119.

far as I know it has not been developed much beyond the
point that the dream image, as a metaphor, does not disguise but reveals a relationship between two elements of
the dream (if someone in a dream is piggish, the dream
will produce a pig, and so on).[3] But this is a narrow conception of the metaphorical process, and when metaphor is
put in the company of its close relatives—metonymy, synecdoche, and irony, the so-called master tropes—we have
an even more complicated problem. To return to my earlier question—in what ways might dreaming be like the
thinking we do when awake?—we find in these tropes the
common strategies by which the work of thought gets
done in and out of poetry. If I may amend I. A. Richards,
tropes "are instances of laws,"[4] and the laws are those that
govern the production of thought. In fact, above all it is
essential to explain that I am concerned not with figures of
speech per se, but with the mental events for which their

[3]I can offer only a sampling of work relating the dream to metaphor:
C. Mason Myers, "Metaphors and the Intelligibility of Dreams," *Phi-
losophy and Rhetoric* 2 (Spring 1969): 91–99; Aurel Kolnai, "The Dream
as Artist," *British Journal of Aesthetics* 12 (Spring 1972): 158–162; Harold
G. McCurdy, "Artistic Creation in Dreams," *Georgia Review* 33
(Spring 1979):195–207; Charles Rycroft, *The Innocence of Dreams* (New
York: Pantheon, 1979), esp. pp. 70–97; Stanley R. Palombo, "The
Genius of the Dream," *American Journal of Psychoanalysis* 43 (1983): 301–
313; Richard M. Jones, "Dream and Metaphor" (paper delivered to the
Association for the Study of Dreams International Conference, Ottawa,
Canada, June 23–29, 1986). Finally, the French Freudians, among other
psychoanalytic groups, commonly discuss dreams in terms of a meta-
phoric-metonymic dyad—for example, see Jacques Lacan, "The Insistence of the Letter in the Unconscious," *Structuralism: Yale French Studies* 36–37 (1966): 129, and Jean Laplanche and Serge Leclaire, "The
Unconscious: A Psychoanalytic Study," *Yale French Studies* 48 (1972):
esp. 147ff. The metaphoric-metonymic dyad derives principally from
Roman Jakobson's classic essay, "The Metaphoric and Metonymic
Poles," in *Fundamentals of Language* (The Hague: Mouton, 1975).
[4]I. A. Richards, *The Philosophy of Rhetoric* (London: Oxford University Press, 1976), p. 36.

designated terms are simply our best words. The point is beautifully put by Arthur Quinn: "Writing is not like chemical engineering. We shouldn't learn the figures of speech the way we learn the periodic table of elements. We shouldn't because we are learning not about hypothetical structures in things, but about real potentialities within our language, within ourselves. . . . In fact, the very phrase 'figures of speech' is misleading in its static, passive form. It should be the 'figurings of speech'—or, better yet, simply 'figuring speech.'"[5] To which I would add, the "figurings of thought," for, as Mary Warnock puts it in her *Imagination,* "It now becomes clear (and indeed it was clear all along) that in talking about images we are talking not only about a class of *things which represent,* but about a species of thinking."[6] We might even say that the four master tropes are to the visual thought process what division, subtraction, addition, and multiplication are to basic arithmetic—that is, the ur-processes of conversion. Beyond the coincidence of "fourness," the analogy gets more interesting in that two of these processes, addition and multiplication, are basically processes of expansion, or going quantitatively beyond, and they have this affinity with metaphor and irony, at least in their operational phases (as I hope to show). The other pair is perhaps less tidy, but on the whole one can say that subtraction and division are processes of reduction; use them and you end up with less than you had. This is the basic principle of the most common forms of metonymy and synecdoche. When you use these two tropes you are usually dividing

[5]Arthur Quinn, *Figures of Speech: 60 Ways to Turn a Phrase* (Salt Lake City: Gibbs M. Smith, 1982), p. 2.

[6]Mary Warnock, *Imagination* (Berkeley and Los Angeles: University of California Press, 1978), p. 159. Throughout her provocative study, the reader will find excellent discussions of the dream in relation to imagination.

something from itself (cause from effect, part from whole, etc.) and leaving something behind, whereas with metaphor and irony you are always augmenting something "from the outside." You can also play interesting games with the cross-tensions between the two sets of pairings. Would not addition and multiplication stand in a metaphorical relationship to each other (as in the biblical pleonasm "increase and multiply"), whereas multiplication and division would stand in a relation of opposition, or irony. For instance, if you multiply 10 by 2 you double 10 and get 20; if you want to get back to 10 you simply divide 20 by 2.

Quinn offers still another way of getting figures of speech out of their rhetorical cages. He suggests that there are four ways to misspell a word: you can add something to it, omit something, substitute something, or rearrange its letters. Likewise, he says, you can classify all figures of speech as figures of addition, omission, substitution, or arrangement (p. 20). If you want to deviate from "ordinary usage," these are the possible forms of deviation. I would add (or am I substituting?) that when you make images, either in an artistic medium or in your own mind, or tell a kind of story either to others or to yourself, you are performing all four of these deviations, and probably all at once. Or, to get down to basics, let us say you are standing before an abundant smorgasbord table and you begin selecting dishes. Some you choose out of nutritional convention—a meat, a vegetable, a starch—some because they are your favorites, some out of curiosity, and some for aesthetic reasons (balance of color, texture, etc.). Finally, some you avoid because they are "bad for you," but you choose others instead. You have, in other words, added, omitted, substituted, and arranged. There on your plate you have written a culinary narrative that you will retire to your table and digest, and while you have not exactly been making figures of speech, you have been performing the mental motions out of which they arise. The psyche's hunger for images begins in physiology, with the "instincts" for proportion, continuity, contrast, compatibility, novelty—all the forms of wariness that guide us through the otherness of reality. And in the dream state the "rhetorical" sympathies between body and mind are especially close. Just as the mind thinks about food for the body's sake, so in the dream the body helps plan the menu of the dream. And by "body" I mean not only such discrete physical stimuli as temperature, discomfort, and cramps, but the whole direction and pulse of one's existence.

In short, the mystery of how thought produces images or sequences of images comes down to such operations as these. I do not think we can neatly pair them, one for one, with the four master tropes, just as we cannot draw clear parallels between the individual tropes and the four arithmetic operations. But basically the same energies are distributed over both, or all three spectrums, and we could probably accommodate the Freudian spectrum (at least such operations as condensation, displacement, symbolism, and contradiction) as well. Metaphor could be considered an additive process, as I have done here, but it is also a form of substitution and arrangement, and we could probably say that it omits something in emphasizing its likeness. Metonymy and synecdoche seem to be primarily processes of omission and substitution, but I cannot rule out that they add or rearrange something, if only our perspective on the thing being set into figure. And when we add to all this the possibilities of mixed figures—for example, synecdochic metaphors and ironic metonymies—things get impossibly confused. But the usefulness of the parallels, if not pressed too mathematically, is that they allow us to generalize thought itself as a synthesis of operations that, taken by themselves, can be discussed in fairly discrete terms. My main interest is to get the idea of tropes out of the customary realm of rhetoric and textual analysis and into the figurings of thought itself. To be metaphorical, the mind, awake or asleep, needs ways to multiply, to divide, to subtract, and to add—to tally experience—and the tropical strategies are our clearest approximations of these operations. In effect, my project for the remainder of this book is to describe the dream phenomenon with help from the principles of rhetoric, though I am really talking about something prior to rhetoric, something on which rhetoric was eventually founded. For example, imagine this highly figural text as a dream:

> Ay, but to die, and go we know not where;
> To lie in cold obstruction and to rot;
> This sensible warm motion to become
> A kneaded clod, and the delighted spirit
> To bathe in fiery floods, or to reside
> In thrilling region of thick-ribbed ice;
> To be imprison'd in the viewless winds,
> And blown with restless violence round about
> The pendant world. . . .
> (*Measure for Measure*, 3.1.118–126)

—that is, imagine it not as a felicitous union of images ("thrilling region," "viewless winds," etc.) but as the thing itself, projected all around you on the canopy of the mind, taken as reality because it is unmediated by the distractions of reality or by a category of disbelief. Dreams rarely get this rowdy, and when they do we call them nightmares. But this freedom to confuse categories was the metaphorical basis of dreaming long before we knew what a metaphor was. So, in applying the tropes to dreaming, we are really speaking about what a metaphor or a metonymy or a synecdoche or an irony might be like if you were trapped inside of one—or worse, if they were all coming at you at once.

My sense and definition of the tropes differs considerably from that of the psychoanalysts, particularly the French Freudians, who accept as given the notion of the unconscious and are therefore concerned only with the linguistic basis of distortion and censorship. That is, because any tropical operation constitutes in some sense a displacement, all tropes (principally metaphor and metonymy) become the mechanism, or site, of a repression. Carrying this claim to its extreme seems to cast human thought into an endless aporia in which all analogy and association are nothing but strategies of self-deception. Of course, one rarely knows how extreme the claim actually is, but it seems reasonable to assume that metaphor (for example), like any operation of mind, is itself neutral to the will and occurs in all designs of thought. To put it another way, when something is said something else is not said. And the nature of your project determines whether you will see the "not said" as an *un*-said—that is, as a repression—or simply as being outside the significance of what is expressed. Without denying the validity of the former, I want to concentrate on the implications of the latter. In short, I take the following remarkable statement by Laplanche and Leclaire at face value: "If analysis seeks to elucidate what it means to speak, it must also at times be the case that speech *means* . . . what it says."[7] Or, to transfer this idea to the dream, we need metaphors and tropes not to disguise meanings but to express meanings that are inexpressible in purely verbal terms.

The master tropes alone, of course, do not offer a com-

[7]Laplanche and Leclaire, "The Unconscious," p. 126.

plete taxonomy of dream strategies. Most rhetorical devices have their equivalents in the dream-work because they are first and foremost strategies of expressiveness before they are figures of speech. For example, there is a hyperbolic quality about dreams in that they seem to carry things to extremes. Dreams pun, as everyone from Freud onward realizes; they use oxymorons, paradoxes, and ellipses, synesthesia and catachresis (e.g., "blind mouths"), prosopopoeia (personification), and so on. But the master tropes, so called for good reasons, do more of the fundamental work of dreams between them than all the other tropes, most of which are subspecies of one or another of the master tropes themselves. So, to avoid tediousness in exampling other figures, let us say that they will allow us to approximate in familiar terms the imaginative means by which the brain thinks images out of feelings and then converts these images to other images along paths of likelihood—likelihood that has almost nothing to do with what we expect to encounter in the waking world.

4 *Metonymy and Synecdoche*

FOR REASONS I hope to make clear, I see metaphor and metonymy as primary strategies, to which I would add, respectively, synecdoche and irony as adjunct modifiers. We have, then, two main dream processes: the metonymic-synecdochic and the metaphoric-ironic. To some extent, this is consistent with modern theory from Jakobson through Lacan, Genette, and Laplanche, all of whom oppose metaphor and metonymy as primary tropes. Where I diverge most obviously is in my conception of these tropes, particularly metonymy, and in my conjunction of metaphor and irony as sister tropes. I ask the reader to remember throughout that my separate treatment of the tropes is strictly a matter of convenience in description. Brain activity takes place at such incredible speed that, were it possible, we would "hear" only the steady hum of the dream machine and not the rattle of its separate parts that you will be hearing here. In fact, before turning directly to metonymy it will be useful to have a better overall view of the dream process as it involves the role of figures in image formation.

My sense is that the dream is a reciprocating machine that "teaches" itself as it goes. It does not think ahead, as

writers do, but feels its way on a principle of self-con-
sistency that I will eventually place under the aegis of synecdoche. Following Gerald Edelman, I suggest that the
dream is Darwinian in its construction. But what exactly
does this mean? In essence, Edelman maintains that the
brain does not store memory in chunks, as you might
expect in recalling a memory from your past; no single
piece of information is stored in a single place in the brain.
Instead, incoming stimuli are distributed throughout an
exquisite system of neuronal maps that can "speak" to
each other over great brain distances. Thus one map can
borrow information from another to form new informa-
tional categories, somewhat as neighbors borrow sugar or
flour for their own culinary projects. This infinite versatility in the function of memory units is what makes it
possible for us to perform the simple task of substituting
one tool for another that we do not have (on the basis of
structural similarity) and so on up through complex tasks
of motor and intellectual adaptation. Thus the brain is a
tropological machine. Not only can it recall things more
or less as they happened (though nothing is stored simply
as itself), it is also capable of transporting whole memory
systems in selected parts, it can condense emotions and
abstractions into images, and it can find resemblances in
categories that are miles apart. These capacities are what
enable the organism to adapt to unexpected changes in its
environment. Hence, memory is Darwinian in its operation and construction, and given this indispensable versatility of the brain's survival mechanisms, one can immediately see, among other things, the naiveté of assuming
that all long or recessed objects in dreams are sexual in
their symbolism. It all depends on which maps are involved in the transaction.[1]

[1]Much of Gerald Edelman's work is beyond the scope of the layman.
The two most useful essays are his "Through a Computer Darkly:

It seems reasonable to assume that the dream is organized along the same lines—that is, the dream is not programmed in advance or rigidly directed by a motive, and it is certainly not censored. It does not "know" what it is going to do next, but as a quality-seeking or theme-seeking mechanism, it "knows" the *kind* of thing it will do next. The dream has a certain adaptability to both incoming stimuli and what we may refer to as its own discoveries (not to mention, once again, its possible "errors") in progress. Like an organism, the dream can capitalize on variations entering its field from without (an alarm, a siren) and those proceeding from within (memory, the day-residue), and it does this primarily by summoning associations from different maps.

Let us examine a simple fragment of a dream, but to make the illustration more relevant, let us take a clearly tropological moment in which the dream suddenly shifts gears, moving from one scene or set of characters to another. In the diagram below, circle A stands for any dream event. Of course, we cannot really speak of an event as something with borders because a dream flows continuously, like a stream. But for convenience let us think of it in solid-state terms. Graphically, a shift in narrative progress might look like this:

Group Selection and Higher Brain Function," *Academy of Arts and Sciences Bulletin* 36 (October 1982): 20–49, and "Neural Darwinism: Population Thinking and Higher Brain Function," *How We Know,* ed. Michael Shafto (San Francisco: Harper & Row), 1985, pp. 1–30. The theory of Darwinian memory is fully explained in Edelman's recent book, *Neural Darwinism: The Theory of Neuronal Group Selection* (New York: Basic Books, 1987). Edelman's work is beautifully summarized by Israel Rosenfield in "Neural Darwinism: The New Memory Theory," *New York Review of Books,* October 9, 1986, pp. 21–27, and in *The Invention of Memory: A New View of the Brain* (New York: Basic Books, 1988) esp. pp. 177–195.

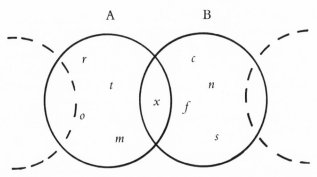

This happens to be a more-or-less standard diagram for metaphorical action, and indeed metaphor is one of the processes we are involved in here. Event A leads to event B through *x*, the area of overlap in the two circles where the metaphor happens; this is at once the site of causality and resemblance. Event A consists of several features (*r*, *t*, *o*, *m*, and of course *x*) that constitute the scene. To make it specific, let us say I am dreaming of a woman sipping wine alone in a dimly lit café; she is mysteriously distant, wears a Garbo hat and gloves, and has long hair. Among these features, let us say that the hat (*x*) is the most dominant, for reasons only the dream would know. But the hat is not simply a hat, any more than the woman is simply a wom-an. In the Darwinian world of the brain, all images carry traces of a history of variation and adaptation, and hats alone must form a complex and ever-changing network of associations. So it is not really a *thing* that reminds us of another thing; it is a thing in a special context, an affective structure, that provokes an associative leap. I might stare all day at my lawn and be reminded of nothing, but if in late afternoon a tree casts its shadow on a rock in a certain way, I might instantly be "carried away" to another scene. In other words, the metaphorical trigger must be an image strong enough to call forth something that is already a metonymy or a synecdoche in another affective pattern.

As C. K. Ogden and I. A. Richards put it, "When a context has affected us in the past the recurrence of merely a part of the context will cause us to react in the way in which we reacted before."[2] It is important to add, however, that in a dream what is called forth by the trigger is not a specific memory, or at least not all of one. Dream memory is not like Proustian memory, in which the whole of one's hometown springs to life from a single cup of tea. The dream is not interested in memories as such, only in making new memories out of the parts of old ones. The dreamer is in the situation of the Scrabble player who plays the game by forming new words, which he can do only by using parts of the words already on the board (the dream in progress) or the random and unique set of letters dealt to him in the draw (the contents of memory). This is another way of saying that the dream thinks like a poet.

In conclusion, however, the hat in the present dream, resonating its peculiar energy, re-minds the dream of something else (another hat, another woman, another café) that is itself an amalgam of memory parts, and the dream evolves to its next event, B, which in its turn contains a potential for narrative development (c, n, f, s). This is a strong shift in dream events. For the most part, dreams have a remarkable narrative stability, and this one may have chosen to remain in the same café with the same woman wearing the same hat. Even in the case I have described, the shift from A to B would very likely take the form of a subtle fusion of my femme fatale with another woman (as in my dream about my mother), thus producing, for the nonce, a composite identity—or (what this lady promised to be all along) a double-agent. But this is a

---

[2]C. K. Ogden and I. A. Richards, *The Meaning of Meaning: A Study of the Influence of Language upon Thought and of the Science of Symbolism* (New York: Harcourt, Brace & World, 1946), p. 53.

matter more appropriate to my discussion of metaphor.

In metonymy the strategy is, in Kenneth Burke's words, "to convey some incorporeal or intangible state in terms of the corporeal or tangible"[3] (as when we speak of "the heart" instead of the emotions, or, in the case of the young man's dream, a faucet instead of the state of sexual excitement). This is a somewhat specialized notion of metonymy. While most definitions of the trope acknowledge its reductive capacity, the emphasis is usually on the principle of causality (cause for effect, effect for cause) or of contiguity (spatial or temporal proximity), or even on contingency (the accidental connection between the figure and what it signifies). This so-called classical definition of metonymy is perfectly compatible with the Burkean idea I shall endorse here. For example, in classical metonymy one might substitute the cause for the effect, the agent for the instrument, the producer for the product, and so on and vice versa, on the basis of contiguity or coexistence in the same context. And thus in a dream one might conjure a person who stands for a locale, a building that stands for a person or a time of life, or an object that stands for the person who owned it. These would all be instances of metonymic (or in some such cases synecdochic) relationships, and I see no reason not to retain them as possibilities. Burkean metonymy behaves in essentially the same way. Because for Burke a metonymy implicitly contains the class of which it is a reduction, it may in turn call forth other members of the class as the dream progresses. The class itself would serve as a repository of variations and substitutes should the dream be interested in "ramifying" (as Burke would say) its original choice. For example, if the dream metonymically reduces your fear of a

---

[3]Kenneth Burke, "Four Master Tropes," *A Grammar of Motives and a Rhetoric of Motives* (Cleveland, Ohio: World, 1962), p. 506.

possible automobile accident involving a loved one, you may, as the dream develops, encounter variations of other such accidents involving other people. Or the dream may elect to move in an adjacent direction to other kinds of endangerment to the same person. In any case, the dream would be calling up reserve episodes that "worry" the original emotion. This would be a case of classical contiguity and Burkean reduction meeting in a common dream project, though I am sure Burke would want to assign some of these transformations to synecdochic "representation."

I prefer Burke's concept of metonymy, not in the interest of restricting it on rhetorical grounds, but because it offers the most fruitful application to the dream process. Metonymy is a form of reduction, whether this involves causality or contiguity or contingency, and it moves, as Burke says, in "but one direction." For example, one could move metonymically from quality to quantity, or from a noncorporeal entity to a corporeal entity, but not from quantity to quality (p. 509n). One can immediately see the affinities of this operation with Freud's principle of condensation, which is an invaluable principle even if you disagree with Freud's notion of its function in the dreamwork. The basic action of metonymy is similar to that of condensation. As the dream thought, or (as I prefer to call it) dream feeling, descends demiurgically from the abstraction of nonsensory thought, we have a metonymic condensation of psychic energy into images that can be "seen" by the brain and used to make dreams (or, in waking life, to build concepts or to solve problems). Metonymy, for present purposes, is the operation by which the brain produces the image that marks the onset of the dream proper and thereafter any scenic shift in substance or theme that might be provoked by the dream in progress.[4] As Werner

[4] A good comprehensive text on the subject of how images descend from abstraction is Rudolf Arnheim's *Visual Thinking* (Berkeley and

and Kaplan put it, this shift

> begins with a phase in which meanings are felt or suffered
> rather than cognitively apprehended. The earliest represen-
> tations are presumed to be of an affective-sensory-motor
> nature, representations which serve perhaps to establish
> global outlines of the experience but which do not establish
> circumscribed connotations or lead to an articulation and
> inner organization of the total experience. Gradually, the
> diffuse and interpenetrating sentiments and meanings gain
> some degree of embodiment in personal, idiomatic, and
> contextualized gestures or images.[5]

One can get a clearer idea of what this process may entail
from the hypnagogic interval preceding sleep in which we
"metonymically" experience the onset of images ex ni-
hilo. Any student of dreams knows that all that is required
to produce these images is a state of passive receptivity to
the shifting play of light and shade on the brain's blank
optical screen. Here there must be a good deal of collusion
between the eye and the imagination, because one can lie
in the dark with nothing in mind and coax vague shapes,
even pinpoints of entoptic light, into the remarkable
sharpness of a face or a landscape you will never see in this
world. Of course, the hypnagogic image is not a dream,
and dreaming does not necessarily follow from it. What
gives birth to these images beyond involuntary physiolog-

Los Angeles: University of California Press, 1969).

[5]Heinz Werner and Bernard Kaplan, *Symbol Formation: An Organismic-Developmental Approach to Language and the Expression of Thought*
(New York: Wiley, 1963), p. 242; this quotation occurs in the chapter
entitled "Handling of Linguistic Forms in Dreams" (pp. 240–252),
which is especially interesting in its analysis of "dream speech" as being
"quite close to an extreme condition of *inner speech,* where the boundary
between self as addressor and self as addressee is scarcely established"
(p. 241).

ical stimulae (retinal excitation, body temperature, muscular contractions, etc.) we do not know, but surely here we are getting a preview, while awake, of how dreams reduce energy to imagery.

Sartre remarks that hypnagogic images, unlike dream images proper, always occur in isolation, without a world. They "have no past, no future, there is nothing behind them or alongside of them."[6] I am not sure of this, or at least I have had preoneiric images that seem to form a world, under certain conditions (for example, if I become *interested* in the image), and go on to become what I can only call nocturnal daydreams in which I fall asleep while returning to my home town, and so on, and somewhere along the line I begin to dream. But Sartre's distinction between the hypnagogic and the dream image offers a useful way to explain the dynamic quality of the dream image, which, he says, comes to the sleeping person as an inherently *participial* energy. For example, the action of my dream about the snake in the forest (Chapter 1) might be summed up participially as "seeing-enemy-snake-as-friend." That is, the image itself is always the seedling of an action; it refers to "a before and an after" and "appears on a foundation of a very rich spatial field" (p. 216). Because the dream is at bottom always an "imitation" of durational experience, or praxis, the dream image never occurs as a "still life" or a static ensemble of features, but as a pictorial *act,* or verb, that is off and running the moment it drops into view.

The obvious advantage of thinking of dream images as metonymic reductions is that it gets us away from the notion that all images are referring to something that is not permitted to appear. A metonymy is something that con-

---

[6]Jean-Paul Sartre, *The Psychology of Imagination,* trans. Bernard Frechtman (New York: Washington Square Press, 1968), p. 216.

veys in its very form a complex significance that could in many cases not be unraveled without access to all the stored experience in the brain's neural library. Consequently, we have no problem now with Wittgenstein's complaint, because it is not a matter of *smuggling past* but of *bringing to*. But symbolic thinking is difficult to overcome. For example, Jonathan Winson, in his argument against Freud's notion of censorship, quite plausibly sees dream distortion "not as a defense but as a reflection of the normal associative process by which experience is interpreted and integrated" by the brain.[7] He refers to this process as "feature detection" and uses as his example two dreams of a thirteen-year-old girl named Emily, first recorded by David Foulkes in a Wyoming clinic in the 1970s. In the first dream, Emily dreams of a choker that had somehow been left in the street. Her girlfriend tries to retrieve it for her, but her girlfriend's father, in whose car they are riding, drives away, leaving her stranded. In the second dream, a month later, Emily dreams of "a choker or bracelet or something" being passed around by "a bunch of girls" in a small room. Winson agrees with Foulkes' notion that the choker represents the idea of "shared femininity" and that there is no censorship at work here, only an expressiveness: "Representing the vagina as itself would not suffice, for where would the sharing appear? Emily's associative process arrived at a natural solution—the choker had the basic shape of the female sexual organ, was associated with females by its use, and could be pictured in the dream as shared" (p. 215).

My only hesitation about this reading concerns what the choker is doing in the dream. I am unable to see why a vagina has anything to do with the dream, apart from the

[7]Jonathan Winson, *Brain and Psyche: The Biology of the Unconscious* (Garden City, N.Y.: Doubleday, 1985), p. 214.

fact that if Emily had not been a female child she would have had no desire for a choker. But that does not mean that the choker refers to her vagina or that femininity necessarily takes a vaginal shape in dream imagery. This is biology with a vengeance. The choker is probably precisely what it is, a prized object worn by young girls, round in shape because it is worn around the neck, standing only for its beauty and for what conventional values usage has given it. It is what gets lost and "passed around" by young girls. In other words, a great many "incorporeal" assumptions about female behavior are tangibly summed up in the choker; as a metonymic carrier of these assumptions, it takes the place of nothing and is a substitute for nothing. It gets into the dream much as a thirteen-year-old boy might dream of an air rifle or a pony because they summed up the entire mythology of the cowboy, and not in the least because they represented his penis. We must grant that, in cases where the image is overdetermined and accompanied by an erotic affect, a rifle or a choker would carry an explicit sexual charge, but that does not appear to be the case in Emily's dream.

The metonymic condensation of feeling into image would be the critical first stage of the dream process, but we must now add the services of metonymy's fellow trope—synecdoche—in order to account for a further dimension of the process. Unfortunately, there is even more confusion about metonymy and synecdoche than about any of the other tropes. Some theorists consider synecdoche a subform of metonymy, others reverse the emphasis. What we can say with some assurance is that both tropes are forms of reduction whereby ambiguities and totalities are dissolved into portable substances. In general, I agree with Albert Henry that "metonymy and synecdoche are modalities of a single fundamental figure: a figure of focalization and contiguity. They are not different in their logic, but in their field of application."[8] It is the difference in the field of application that will concern me here.

Synecdoche, in Burke's definition, overlaps on metonymy in the sense that "a reduction is [also] a representation" (p. 507) in which the part represents the whole, the whole the part, the cause the effect, and so on.[9] As I am thinking of the two tropes here, metonymy is basically a *qualitative* reducer of attributes into conventional emblems (authority into scepter, girlhood into choker), and synecdoche is basically a *quantitative* reducer of unified systems into representative units, usually those that are the most visually functional in the whole (ships into sails, sailors into hands). It is generally agreed that metonymy and synecdoche are figures of contiguity as well as of reduction and representation—that is, *as* reductions, they remain within a single spatial, temporal, or conceptual domain (crown and king, things that happen on the same day, things existing in the same mental context). Unlike metaphor, they do not import "foreign bodies" into their referential systems. Thus, to speak of the heart in terms of the emotions would be metonymical not only because it reduces an intangible to a tangible but also because heart belongs (like the crown to the king) to the person having the emotions. The same principle would apply if one synecdochically reduced ships

8Albert Henry, *Métonymie et métaphore* (Paris: Klincksieck, 1971), p. 26.

9For Burke, the cause-effect relationship belongs to synecdoche rather than to metonymy. Burke attributes many of the classical metonymic relationships to synecdoche, which for him is *the* master trope, or trope of all tropes—for example, "The more I examine both the structure of poetry and the structure of human relations outside of poetry, the more I become convinced that this is the 'basic' figure of speech, and that it occurs in many modes besides that of the formal trope" (*The Philosophy of Literary Form* [New York: Random House, 1957], p. 23).

to sails. On the other hand, to speak of the emotions as a furnace or a cauldron would be metaphorical because you have jumped to another domain of reference that has nothing (except heat) to do with the emotions. Metonymy and synecdoche, then, are the stay-at-home tropes, and as mental operations they are concerned with keeping things in their place. There is something conservative or "traditional" about metonymy and synecdoche, at least as they occur in figural language. They do not die easily, like metaphors and ironies, but become "best words" for reducing things. For example, "the head" and "the heart" are still valid names for reason and passion, and one would never think of saying "Here come twenty rudders or twenty riggings" as a way of saying something fresh about approaching ships. This does not mean that we cannot discover new metonymies or synecdoches or that they are always forms of established shorthand; it only means that the very movement of the two strategies is a movement *within* a circle of implications, and this is what gives rise to an emblematic or iconic value. Altogether, metonymy and synecdoche are ways of naming, whereas metaphor and irony are ways of un-naming or re-naming. This is simple to say, but the lines of distinction among the three tropes sometimes virtually disappear. As Albert Henry says, there is something faintly metonymic about all metaphors, and something faintly metaphorical about all metonymies (p. 50).

There are probably all sorts of synecdochic designs in dreams, such as when I find myself literally driving down the freeway on a set of wheels, or when I find I have gone on vacation with only a toothbrush—in other words, any situation in which a part of something is doing the work of the whole. But I am more interested in the overall sense in which the dream is representative of the psychic "system" of the dreamer. "Artistic representation," Burke says, "is synecdochic, in that certain relations within the medium 'stand for' corresponding relations outside it." Moreover, the work itself is "internally synecdochic . . . , the parts all . . . being consubstantially related."[10] If we are thinking of the dream as a mode of artistic representation in which the dreamer's psychic experience is somehow "imitated" and correlated with prior experience, then the dream is synecdochically a part of the larger outside whole of the dreamer's psychic life—which is being continually amended and updated by the process of representative reduction—and it is also internally consistent in that all its parts are related. To put it another way, the business of the dream-work is to preserve the *quality* of a certain experience by seeing that it is *quantitatively* represented by the appropriate parts. The dream must add up to the feeling of which it is the carrier. This may seem to verge on tautology, but one of the things that tends to be forgotten by both theorists and dreamers is that the dream is composed before the dreamer's very eyes. How is it that the dreaming brain can so instantaneously create a world, people it, and involve the people so complicitously in what is after all a subjective fiction? Must we not assume that one of the innate capacities of the brain is something *like* a synecdochic intuition, a sensitivity to wholeness in the presence of a part and partness in the presence of a whole? And we might expand this idea along the following lines:

What is inherently pleasing to the mind is a sense of coherence in a perceived whole, of things somehow coming together in a demonstration of unity. "We experience many things," Lakoff and Johnson say, "through sight and touch, as having distinct boundaries, and, when things have no distinct boundaries, we often project boundaries upon them—conceptualizing them as entities and often as containers."[11] For example, when we confront the assault

[10]Burke, *A Grammar of Motives*, p. 508.
[11]George Lakoff and Mark Johnson, *Metaphors We Live By* (Chicago: University of Chicago Press, 1980), p. 58.

of the sea on a segment of shoreline or a cloud formation building in the sky, we intuitively find the center of the drama and project boundaries on it. Or, in looking at poor art we sense how certain parts do not belong or belong improperly to each other. On the positive side, our enjoyment in viewing well-executed art has to do with our impression of wholeness inhabiting the parts, and vice versa. Art imitates the action of things, rather than the things themselves, and actions are primarily wholes. Synecdochically, then, we frame the world through the most natural of acquired perceptual habits. The Sunday photographer, carefully locating his subject through the viewfinder, is modestly in search of what the mathematician more elegantly calls a "golden ratio," a perfect relationship between parts and whole. So as I am thinking of it here, the synecdochic operation is not simply a sail-for-ship substitution. Synecdoche is always a seed, or germ cell, that carries a set of instructions, or even better a structuration in which a wholeness inheres. It is the principle of coherence writ small. In the world of rhetoric we have always had trouble keeping synecdoche and metonymy apart, and some rhetoricians even collapse them into each other. But we probably do this because they are co-assistants in the same work of birthing the image. As Burke would say, they are "special applications" of the same operation. Metonymy's primary business is reification; synecdoche's is coherence, and it is analogous to the artist's instinct for fullness of expression, or "getting all the right things in."

I do not want to create the impression that the synecdochic element in dreams is in any way similar to the conscious control exercised by the artist over his materials. The dream-work does not have "good taste," though something bordering on taste inheres in a dream (for example, through the dream we learn that we have retained far more of the subtlety of our experience than we realized). Moreover, when we speak of the whole-part relationship in dreams we are not referring to wholes in the Aristotelian sense of things that have beginnings, middles, and endings. The wholeness of the dream is simply its adequacy as a container of feeling. The dream is efficient, whatever its purposes; it never falls into the redundancies and trivialities one would find in most dreamers' waking attempts at fiction. No one understood better than Freud the precise self-sufficiency of the dream to elaborate a content based on experience but never (or at least rarely[12]) a duplication of experience. What the dream duplicates is the structure of experience, and this is the respect in which the precise nature of the parts is less important than the role they play.

This can best be illustrated with an example. I assume that a relatively common dream pattern involves what I might participially refer to as "getting-acquainted-in-a-new-place." In waking life this is a condition of exposure over time (as when we "get to know" someone or "learn to like" a place). To know something is to be able to re-recognize it, but in dreams the sensation of "knowing" someone or some place occurs instantaneously, as a fait accompli. For example, on one of my dream-streets I might suddenly recognize an old friend I knew years ago ("Aren't you—X?") who bears no resemblance to the friend in question. It is possible that the dream-character has certain features similar to X's or that he is a composite identity, but this is not always the case, and we are left with the interesting phenomenon of recognizing someone we do not recognize (as in our earlier case of the stranger-

---

[12]However, Freud reports cases in which the dream reproduces events exactly as the dreamer perceived them in waking life (*SE* 4:21). This is an unprovable claim, but at most such dreams would seem to be a rare phenomenon.

mother). Now, suppose I have a dream in which I find myself in a new place where I have taken a job. There are no old friends here, and I am in the process of meeting people. I know A and B rather well from the interviews, correspondence, and one or two social occasions (A seems to have been my sponsor); X and Y I know less well, and I am now introduced (at a party in my honor) to Z for the first time. Shortly, Y approaches to tell me something helpful about the place. I am embarrassed because I have forgotten his name, and I make a mental note to ask A—or better still, C, the department secretary, who seems to be the kind of person who would understand my lapse. All these people, barely five minutes old by the dream-clock, exude that abundant geniality that comes with wanting to put the new person at ease. Yet they are all distinct and precisely individuated, down to facial expressions and mannerisms (Y's odd laugh, A's powerful handshake), even to the way C, an attractive woman in her thirties, quietly oversees the group like a hostess giving a party. But each one has been freshly minted for this occasion, and I shall never see them again in future dreams.

Apart from any immediate tensions that may have produced the dream, what is happening here amounts to a sensory paradox in which the brain seems to be playing tricks with itself. How can I feel the sensation of varying degrees of familiarity with these people I have never met—who do not in fact exist—unless the sensation itself, in all its complexity, has synecdochically produced the people who are simply representative of it? What my dream must surely be amplifying, or drawing on, is my personal history in these situations. It has caught the perceptual dimensions of the "getting acquainted" experience perfectly by creating people who form a model of all such new people in new places in my past. These are the parts it takes to make up the whole of such an experience. Not precisely this number, but *these kinds*. In fact, because there are usually several anonymous people hovering about at such functions, my dream has thoughtfully provided a number of extras to round out the scene, one of whom looks suspiciously at me from across the room as if I were not the right person for the job. The truly remarkable thing is how the dream can summon the necessary parts that will constitute the whole experience. The scene is not an imitation, in the sense of copy; it is a complete invention based on an elaborate process of associational searching and "feature detection." To anyone who has undergone the scene several times, it is archetypal, and "archetype" is another term for the whole that lies behind and inheres in all the parts, which turn out to be infinitely replaceable.

The mission of synecdoche, then, is to confine the dream to an orderly pursuit of its theme, to which each of its parts strives to make its contribution. This is not to argue that dreams are always orderly, but to marvel that they achieve an expressiveness that could not be duplicated in the most serene of daydreams. It is impossible to separate out the precise operations and limits of metonymy and synecdoche in such cases, but it seems reasonable to say that there is, on one hand, the immediate factor of the birth of the image out of the dream feeling and, on the other hand, the integrative or genetic factor that sculpts and controls the image as the offspring of the dreamer's personal history. In this connection it is useful to recall an underrated characteristic of the dream—it has no interest in reconstructing a specific experience from the dreamer's past, or even a fresh one it will select as the day-residue of tonight's dream. The original experience, which is stored in the memory as perceived and certainly available to partial recall, is all but irrelevant in itself. And, indeed, why should the dream repeat the history of the dreamer when all its mechanisms are precisely those of conversion and reduction rather than imitation and description? What the dream offers instead is a fictitious formula of the experience in which the dreamer relives the experience's emotional contours but not the experience itself. The abandoned barn on the hill in which I played as a boy and can to this day recall perfectly in my mind's eye is of no concern to my dream as a precise place it will take me to tonight in my nostalgic mood. It will take me to a barn of its own. Yet I shall find myself back *there* again, because the particular doors, ladders, and lofts that I remember were only the given conditions of my contentment there. Only in the familiarity, the taken-for-grantedness, did the contentment that would become the subject of a future night's dream arise. It is not the barn I shall find familiar, but the emotion of my contentment in it, and this is what will lend to my new dream's image the status of the old place. And so it is that a "false" image can stand in for the real one with no loss of verisimilitude. The dream image is not a memory deformed, but a feeling reconstituted out of the chance blocks of form available to my brain on an instant's notice on a particular night.

Before I move on to the metaphorical phase, it remains to say something about the psychic force behind the metonymic reduction. What is this intangible that is made tangible by the dream? Like most dream theorists, I assume that the dream is not arbitrarily inspired and that it is not accidental that I have a particular dream on a particular night. For Freud the dream originates in the dream-thoughts—always a repressed wish that is somehow connected to the day-residue. Moreover, Freud argued that the affect, or emotional tone, of the dream has an undependable relationship to the manifest content, which has always undergone displacement—that is, in a dream we may be frightened by something trivial and remain unconcerned in the face of something normally fearful (for example, my snake dream in Chapter 1). Freud explained this apparent paradox by saying that the dream-work is either suppressing the affect, deviating it to another part of the dream, compromising two opposing affects, or turning a single affect into its opposite.[13] This is a necessary corollary to the theory of repression, and I return to it in my chapter on irony. Here I simply advance my own sense of what may be taking place between affect and dream-thought.

Let me begin with an example of an apparent paradoxical affect. I periodically have a dream in which my friends and family gather at the shore to see the high waves rising during a storm at sea. The dream is always vivid and pleasant, and it follows roughly the same pattern: the waves grow to ominous heights until they wash over us all, but no one gets wet or drowned. In almost every dream I suffer my own personal wave, which rises from the sea like the monstrous bull in *Hippolytus* and, suffused with awareness of me, spills onto the land and inundates me. Again, there is no pain or terror—or rather, there is the exhilarated "terror" of the child who knows that his uncle, playing the monster, will not hurt him in a game of "get you." Here indeed is the perfect wave, born of all those occasions on which I have waited in vain for the truly big one, the mountainous wave that carries to the extreme the sublime potentiality of water. As the instrument of my will, I have imagined it as I want it to be— which is not a guarantee of dreams but one of their possibilities. In short, there is a sympathy between the terrifying and the self that requires no disguise. What is frightening in one dream may be pleasurable in another, depending on the thoughts that have given rise to the dream. But

[13]Freud's discussion of these ideas is found in "Affects in Dreams," *SE* 5:460–487.

in all dreams the affect is a direct expression of the emotional origins of the dream.

Unfortunately, it is impossible to define these origins or to describe their limits, because we have no access to the preparatory and nonsensory phase of the dream. The term I prefer for them over Freud's "dream-thoughts" is "dream-feelings," primarily because it carries an emotional (as opposed to cognitive) connotation that accompanies most dreams—or so I believe. In any case, a dream-feeling is not simply an emotion, like fear, joy, anger, or grief. It must be something that is susceptible to dream narration and can itself be reciprocally altered by the dream, for it seems evident that a dream *discovers* its subject as it evolves, at least within certain synecdochic boundaries. As I see it, a dream-feeling is almost identical to what Bartlett calls an attitude, which, he says, is "largely a matter of feeling, or affect."[14] An attitude is "an interplay of appetites, instincts, interests and ideals" (p. 213) that is being continually altered by incoming experience. And because the dream is a species of memory recall, we may say that, like remembering, it is "then a construction, made largely on the basis of this attitude, and its general effect is that of a justification of the attitude" (p. 207), or perhaps we may say that the dream is the embodiment of the attitude, or what I am calling a feeling. Finally, my sense of feeling, with some qualification, might include one advanced by Ricoeur: "Feelings . . . have a very complex kind of intentionality. They are not merely inner states but interiorized thoughts. It is as such that they accompany and complete the work of imagination as schematizing a synthetic operation: they make the schematized thought ours. . . . Feeling is not contrary to thought. It is thought made ours."[15] Or, with respect to

[14]Bartlett, *Remembering*, p. 207.

[15]Paul Ricoeur, "The Metaphorical Process as Cognition, Imagination, and Feeling," *Critical Inquiry* 5 (Autumn 1978): 156.

dreaming, perhaps we should say that feeling is what produces the schematized image. Ricoeur says that when we *feel*, we are "assimilated, that is, made similar, to what is seen as similar. . . . We feel *like* what we see *like*" (p. 156). Ricoeur is of course referring to our exposure to poetic imagery, not to our involuntary production of dream images. Should we not say, then, that in the dream state we produce images similar to our feelings, we dream *like* what we feel *like?* Or, to return to my dream, I have made a wave that is similar to my feeling.

In any event, the dream-feeling is substantially emotional in character, though sometimes it may appear to be intellectual or rational, as in the problem-solving dream. Let us look briefly at this species of dream, however. The most famous example is probably the dream of the dancing snakes from which Kekule derived the structure of the carbon atom in the benzene molecule.[16] This would seem to be a purely intellectual dream having no reference to anything but the benzene problem Kekule had tried so hard to solve, and in fact had dreamed about many times without success. Frankly, Kekule was lucky, for his failed dreams are far more typical of the species. Problem-*solving* dreams are extremely rare, though problem-*having* dreams are common. Going to sleep with a pressing intellectual problem tends to produce dreams that either repeat the structure of the attempt to solve the problem, often to the

---

[16]C. A. Meier (*The Unconscious in Its Empirical Manifestation, with Special Reference to the Association Experiment of C. G. Jung* [Boston: Sigo Press, 1984], pp. 18–23) argues persuasively that Kekule was not sleeping during the event of his discovery but dozing, the word Kekule actually uses in his account, and that the dancing snake "dream" belongs more properly to the category of hypnagogic vision. It is impossible, obviously, to determine how far into sleep Kekule had gone. The matter does not really affect the point I am making: that problem-solving dreams are rare. Meier also offers an interesting discussion of the emotional quality of Kekule's dream-vision.

point of sleeplessness, or create brilliant solutions that are simply silly in the light of day. More than once, while working on this project, I have taken a particular problem to sleep (for example, the relationship of one dream process to another) and have repeatedly "solved" it by the manipulation of water pipes in my garden drip system, the placement of guests at a dinner table, or an obsessive attempt to push Saturday literally into the middle of the week, on the theory that the week (like my theory?) would be better balanced if the holidays were more evenly distributed between the working days. There is clearly nothing that cannot be converted into a metaphor for the problem. What the dream has pursued, in these cases, is not a rational solution but the elation or the frustration of finding or not finding a solution, and this can be projected onto any structure that will accept it. We dream like what we feel like.

A similar instance occurs in dreams involving the solving of a crime. It seems evident that such dreams are based on the dreamer's familiarity with detective fiction and films, and if it were not afield of my purpose here it would be interesting to pursue the question of how much conventional literary and cinematic forms influence our dreams and in some cases provide the feeling that produces them. Might not fear, mystery, or intrigue, in certain dreams, be the result of having had such feelings induced in us by countless books and films and therefore imprinted in the brain as permanent forms of anticipation? For example, I frequently have a whodunit dream that takes place in a room where several people are gathered following the crime (always vague). There is a detective who interrogates the group and who in due course announces the name of the killer, to everyone's shock. On waking I am astonished at how brilliantly my dream "wrote" the story, leading to the reversal through an orderly pursuit of clues. But it quickly dawns on me that I can recall little about the dream beyond what I have just described and a certain sense of the scene and the placement of now faceless people. What has happened here, I gather, is that my dream has imitated the emotional contour of suspense common to the discovery scene of detective fiction, but the specific content is no more germane to the crime or the solution than my irrigation system was to my intellectual problem, or if there is a connection, it is lost on me. There was no orderly pursuit of clues, simply a series of images on which I had projected the feeling that clues were being pursued, that suspense was mounting, and that the detective's solution, when it came, was correct, though I recalled nothing about the crime or the circumstances surrounding it. Thus we have a phantom content unfolding in a generic emotional structure. An excellent literary illustration of the idea is Ionesco's surrealist play *The Bald Soprano,* which faithfully follows the structure of a drawing-room melodrama but fills it with nonsense and nonsequiturs. The effect is similar to that of watching a television show with the volume turned off, or a foreign film without subtitles—the emotional spectacle is all there, but you cannot tell what is causing it.

I have no desire to exclude a strictly intellectual origin to the dream, though I cannot imagine what that might be. If feeling has a cognitive dimension, it may be because cognition cannot be cleanly separated from the forms of neuronal excitation we call emotions. It is probably true that many scientific problems have been solved with the help of dreams, but in the cases familiar to me the solution does not come in the dream itself. Kekule dreamed of dancing snakes, not the benzene ring; Elias Howe dreamed of being executed by natives with oddly designed spears, not the sewing machine needles he was to conceive as a consequence of the dream, and so on. It is possible that the dream has accidentally provided half of a metaphor, which the dreamer completes on waking. Or it is possible that, as Richards would put it, he finds a *tenor,* or underlying idea, that belongs with the vehicle serendipitously supplied by the dream—much as Kekule might have discovered the benzene principle while blowing smoke rings over morning coffee. In any case, at this point in our understanding of dreams nothing can be served by a dogmatic theory that sets limits on the nature of the dream-feeling. The most we can say is that it seems to be born substantially of our emotional investments, both large and small.

Moreover, it seems presumptuous to assume that dreams serve a single purpose or to limit the latent content of dreams to certain kinds of emotional tension (e.g., sexual) that must be repressed. There is some reason to believe that dreams are not as exclusively centered on our "deep" personal problems as we seem to think. For example, it is typical of dreams to pass over dramatic or influential happenings—an accident, a death, a promotion—and to select something trivial in comparison. That a dream ignores the event of a family funeral need be no more an act of repression than its avoidance of a joyous birth or wedding. It is possible that what the dream chooses as its day-residue are simply points of correlation between experience arriving and experience already there. One recalls that for Proust the past was hidden "somewhere outside the realm, beyond the reach of intellect, in some material object (in the sensation which that material object will give us) which we do not suspect."[17] Following the memory theories of Bartlett and Edelman, we might assume that certain experiences of each day—and it is hopeless to know why these rather than others—must somehow take their place in the memory, not simply by storing them

[17]Marcel Proust, *Swann's Way,* trans. C. K. Scott Moncrieff (New York: Modern Library, 1956), p. 61.

"like so many definite impressions," as Bartlett says, "fix-
ed and having only the capacity of being re-excited,"[18] but
as an attitudinal conformation, that is, as having not only
spatial and temporal specificity but also a qualitative essence. They must be put integrally in the brain as belong-
ing to what is already there. To put it in the current terminology, they must be filed synchronously as well as
diachronically. One way in which dreams might serve this
function involves what we may call (at least for the moment) a synecdochic transformation. In brief, some element of the day experience (a material object perhaps)
triggers a memory of a similar part of another whole belonging to the past. This whole is not a set of chronological events that occurred on a given day in one's eighteenth
year; it is instead a whole formed by many past products of
a similar feeling—a transtemporal, transspatial whole.
And the dream that results from this transformation will
almost invariably have the Parnassian character we have
already spoken about; people, places, and events will be
impossibly mixed yet persistently homotonous.

There is an interesting example of this process of mixing
odd categories in an essay by Roger Schank and Colleen
Seifert. It would probably also serve as an instance of metaphorical transformation, but I offer it here, in the context
of attitude conformation, as a transitional means of summing up one point while pointing toward the next. Schank
and Seifert are basically interested in "how we learn"
through what they call "knowledge structures"—that is,
"some package of information with built-in expectations."[19] The problem facing the brain in processing a

[18]Frederic C. Bartlett, *Remembering: A Study in Experimental and Social Psychology* (Cambridge: Cambridge University Press, 1932), p. 214.
[19]Roger C. Schank and Colleen M. Seifert, "Modeling Memory and
Learning," *How We Know,* ed. Michael Shafto (San Francisco: Harper &
Row, 1985), p. 71.

piece of information is to find a knowledge structure that is sufficiently broad to enable it to make qualitative or attitudinal connections with other things. In the following example, the knowledge structure is what they refer to as "somebody provides service for somebody else":

> X described how his wife would never make his steak as rare as he liked it. When this was told to Y, it reminded Y of a time, 30 years earlier, when he tried to get his hair cut in a short style in England, and the barber would not cut it as short as he wanted it (p. 71).

"The purpose of this kind of index into memory," Schank and Seifert say, "is to compare the next version of an expectation failure with the previous version, so that the expectation can be changed to avoid the failure in the future" (p. 72). If the example were to occur as a dream, it would be a classic instance of "distortion." A scene in which I am being served a steak not cooked to my specifications might suddenly be combined with the absurdity of getting a haircut at the dinner table. But the point of "commonality" (or what is called the *tenor* of a metaphor) between the two things would be absent, or present only as a feeling of annoyance. I would not say to myself, at my dream-table, "This reminds me of a haircut I had in England," but I might just have the feeling that my irritation at getting a poor steak is somehow consistent with my getting a haircut while I pout about the steak.

It goes without saying that many, perhaps most, of these fusions of experience that occur in dreams are beneath explanation. They are simply too subtle to recognize because they may be utterly trivial incidents separated by many years (why, in a dream, should I suddenly drop my sunglasses while crossing a room?). Dreams do not understand; they are what is being understood—that is, arranged, enlarged, classified for future understanding. It might be argued that we do not really learn very much from dreams, in the sense that they make us noticeably wiser, more humble, or more tolerant. But this is a waking concept of learning. Learning, as Schank and Seifert say, begins in "processing incoming experience in terms of particular memories" (p. 79). In short, there must be processes by which the brain digests experience for later use, and it seems plausible that sleep would provide an ideal opportunity for that processing because the circuits of attention are free of incoming signals. We do not learn much through dreams, but we may need dreams in order to learn how to remember. In some respects this is a very Proustian idea of memory: things are simply the conduits of the feelings that happen to accompany them. And thus, quite apart from their shape or conventional symbolism, one might store biscuits, steeples, avenues, melodies, and loose paving stones side by side in the same map of the brain.

Finally, there is one related form of dream content I want to touch on. It is what we might simply refer to as meta-experience, or a set of creatural experiences that require—or at least receive—continual representation in dreams simply because they form the understructure of our existence. They are, we may say, metonymic reductions of the experience of being a self surrounded by otherness. "The world obsesses us even during sleep," Merleau-Ponty writes, "and it is about the world that we dream."[20] I shall take this statement quite literally, but because my purpose here is to be illustrative, I mention only three possible categories of "world-dreaming," any one of which might constitute a chapter in itself.

[20]Maurice Merleau-Ponty, *The Phenomenology of Perception*, trans. Colin Smith (London: Routledge & Kegan Paul, 1962), p. 293.

First, we dream about *the resistance of the world,* or the complicity of objects in blocking the path of our plans. Normally life distracts us from this fact, until the car battery goes dead or we find ourselves gazing at a table as an empty thing that has no name and is nothing but otherness. We see the thing, in short, as part of the world we are *in* rather than part of the world we have *made.* The world lies constantly in wait. Anything can happen. Thus accident, in all its forms, good and bad, opens out onto everything because nothing is exempt from it. Accident is by definition what is concealed until it happens. What accident arouses in us, subliminally, is an awareness that the human value system and the causal series have been randomly aligned—that is, not aligned at all. On the extreme, the continuity of the world includes my natural death, and though every biological precedent establishes my death as a certainty, it will be an accident, to me, when it comes. It is hardly a wonder, then, that in dreams pathways, floors, the earth itself, are unreliable, that vehicles are disobedient, that friends betray us, that systems fail, and that now and then we uncover treasure in the backyard.

Second, we dream of *the spectacle of the world.* Need it be said that man is naturally a lover of vistas, depths, heights, breadths, the retreat of the world before the eye, the approach of the outlandish in nature? We have what Kant called a feeling for the sublime, and it appears to be in keeping with our unrestricted imagination that one of the categories of the dream should be a feeling *of* the sublime—not a symbolic sublime, wherein mountains equal sex, but the sublime as a manifestation of the presence of the world, *its* self-expressiveness or (if the word is not exhausted) its grandeur.

Third, we dream of *the pastness of life.* We live in what the philosophers call the "specious present," whose singular and most frustrating quality is that it cannot be contemplated as such because it is constantly being bumped into the past by once-future events. Our life, then, unfolding on the knife edge of a *now* (in George Mead's phrase), is a continuous growth of a past that, like everything else, is endangered by loss—is in fact already (instantly) a part of "the other." Is it not possible, then, that the dream is our purest response to the pastness of life and its unreclaimable content, and that any figure or event from our past is sufficiently dreamworthy on the grounds that it was symbolic of nothing more than a time of life, one of the fixtures of a particular street?

Why should such basic images of experience require referents or come to us masked as symbols of still other things? What could be more important than the *I am,* the *I was,* the *I will (not) be?* These things speak for themselves and obsess us. They are fundamental and ego-transcendent categories of experience—or, if you prefer, *deeply* egotistic. Of course, such images do not normally constitute entire dreams. Instead, they come to us freely mixed with more immediate contents from the personal, sexual, or neurotic spheres. Dreams may give us two for the price of one—for example, the sublime might piggyback on a dream of the senior prom ("We were all in this vast hall . . ."). No doubt the exaggeration is brought on by the experience that took place, after all, in the high school gym, but it also contains its own meaning and justification, born of our life in the open spaces of the world.

Like many theorists, I am reluctant to draw cleaner distinctions between the synecdochic and the metonymic processes. What I am aiming to recover is some approximation of the complexity of dream formation. Within the dream there is no way to know whether the image has produced the feeling or the feeling the image. This is imagination's version of the chicken-egg problem. In either case, as we shall see directly, when we move by association from one synecdoche (or metonymy) to another synecdoche (or metonymy), we are already in the province of metaphor.

5 Metaphor

THUS FAR my model is operationally Freudian in that it assumes both a manifest and a latent dream content. The latter, in my view, is simply a feeling that gets translated, as Freud says, into a "pictographic script."[1] I am not at all sanguine about my approximation of this process. Even the neuroscientists, who draw elaborate electronic graphs of brain activity, are unclear about what is actually traveling over the circuits and how the visible dream may be working in correlation with subvisual thought processes. Are all dreams products of the same process? If so, does this process ever malfunction (nightmares and night terrors)? Are the dreams of "normal" people different from those of people who are mentally ill? For example, Freud's theory of repression emerged from a clinical situation—might it be valid there and less valid elsewhere?[2]

[1]Freud, SE 4:277.

[2]As an illustration of this possibility, see Richard Corriere et al., "Toward a New Theory of Dreaming," *Journal of Clinical Psychology* 33 (1977): 807–820. Based on a rigorous analysis of 654 dreams of a young man undergoing "feeling therapy," the authors find significant evidence that as a subject becomes more and more expressive of his feelings outside the therapy session, his dreams "shift from symbolic, censored, and indirect expressions of affect to direct feeling expression" (p. 807).

Finally, one wonders whether the content of dreams may not be less significant than the act of dreaming itself. Could dreaming be a sort of clearinghouse or a form of neuronal stretching through which we hypothesize possible experiences based on old or recent experiences? Perhaps we dream because it is the brain's business to revise the world for its own purposes, as it is the body's business to revise the food it consumes. The thought has crossed my mind that dreaming may be something the brain does "for pleasure" while the body is asleep, as jazz musicians play the real music after the customers have gone home. When I say that the brain may dream "for pleasure," I am not referring to a willful or voluntary satisfaction of appetite. Rather, I mean a form of unlimited freedom, as Isak Dinesen puts it, through which "things happen without any interference." One characteristic of daydreaming, or of idle thought of any kind, is an improvisational openness whereby one can let the thoughts come out as they will. When you suspend yourself from empirical reality, from problem-solving, the brain switches to the associative mode and simply plays the field. In the practical world we would say that someone given heavily to associative thinking is scatterbrained. In the dream state it seems to provide the brain with its only sustained opportunity to reinvent reality at the level of its subjective residue.

Some support for this idea, or at least some clarification, is offered in Hans-Georg Gadamer's concept of play and its relation to art. Play, Gadamer suggests, is a "natural process" shared by children, adults, and animals. It is a "to and fro movement . . . without goal or purpose" beyond that of "pure self-presentation."[3] Like art, play comes to rest in itself, the sheer transformation of energy into a

[3]Hans-Georg Gadamer, *Truth and Method* (New York: Crossroad, 1985), p. 94.

structure that "absorbs the player into itself, and thus takes from him the burden of the initiative, which constitutes the actual strain of existence" (p. 94). To remove the idea from any confusion with games or game-playing (also a form of play), one might think of play as a creatural need to submit oneself to a structure that is bracketed off from the practical continuity of existence. Play leads to nothing. It is useful only in the sense of its occurring and playing out the possibilities of play in a given mode.

> [Play] no longer permits of any comparison with reality as the secret measure of all copied similarity. It is raised above all such comparisons—and hence also above the question whether it is all real—because a superior truth speaks from it. . . .
> This gives the full meaning to what we called transformation into a structure. The transformation is a transformation into the true. It is not enchantment in the sense of a bewitchment that waits for the redeeming word that will transform things to what they were, but it is itself redemption and transformation back into true being. In the representation of play, what is emerges (p. 101).

Play and dreaming can be differentiated on various levels (e.g., of consciousness, of material existence), but as a transformation of behavior into a structure—that is, a drama made of the self, an "energeia which has its telos within itself" (p. 101), "a reality that surpasses" the player (p. 98)—the dream shares with play, and with art, the same life-function of putting experience in the mode of "the true." The truth of the dream is not a concept, a lesson, a meaning, a prognosis, a diagnosis, or a referent to something outside it—except in the sense of these being by-products. It is a closure of certain lines of force born of existence in the open world. In the dream we draw the wagons of experience into a circle, thus keeping empirical life at bay while another kind of life begins. Thus one might define the dream, from this point of view, as a pursuit of structure that uses the self as its foundation without any further motive beyond bringing given possibilities to perfection. It is the brain doing what it does best without the impediment of actuality. Perhaps we experience play most subtly in those waking moments in which we find ourselves doodling on paper (that is, structuring nonsense), lining up objects in space along the path of a single eye, tinkering with the rhythms of this and that, and in general "improving on" what one finds idly at hand. For example, skipping stones across a lake would be a kind of dreaming of the body.

Such a speculation is beyond proving, and I introduce it here not as an avenue I shall pursue or as a privileged suspicion, but as a possibility that might, given our relative ignorance, allow us to remain open about what dreams do for us. It might not even be contradictory to say that dreams "work" while they play—that is, that the pure play of dreaming, which has no goal respecting conscious application, also performs the useful service of keeping the organism in good working order (somewhat like tennis or jogging) by stretching neuronal capacities for storage and expressiveness. In other words, the dream may be like a compulsive file-clerk for whom filing is at once both useful (to others) and an end in itself. But what primarily interests me here is not the role of dreams as a carrier of data but the dream as a phenomenon that manifests, under special conditions (sleep), the universal characteristics of thought, particularly imaginative thought. For instance, my eye was immediately caught by Gerald Edelman's discussion of classification, the basic process involved in selective memory: "The problem of classification requires that two conditions be satisfied. The first is to recognize similarities among things in the same class. The second is to recognize differences among things in different classes, as well as among things in the same class."[4] Why not a third condition, I thought, *to recognize similarities among things in different classes?* Perhaps this moves us beyond classification to the realm of reorganization, or perhaps it is covered inversely by the second condition. At any rate, this third condition—by which I mean metaphor—is what makes it possible for me to substitute a rock for a hammer I do not have, my cupped hands for a water glass, a stick for a lever, or to move for any purpose from one classification to another on the basis of likeness. In Edelman's theory there is a fundamental property of the brain called degeneracy, which refers (fortunately) to neural networks that are structurally different but respond similarly to a given stimulus. It is by means of degenerate networks that the brain is able to recognize new things as belonging to old patterns. Without them, generalizations from specifics would be impossible. Thus a degenerate set might resemble a metaphor and perhaps even be built like one in that it would consist of different structures that have something in common. Of course, degenerate sets are not metaphors, but if I say they are *like* metaphors I apparently have to use one or two of them in order to do so. Moreover, what better way to define a metaphor than Edelman's definition of a degenerate network: "a non-isomorphic set of isofunctional structures" (p. 36)? Inelegant perhaps, but it does get us down to fundamentals. Truly, the metaphor, as Ortega y Gasset has said, is "a tool for creation which God forgot inside one of his creatures when he made him."[5] And truly, perhaps we can now take

[4]Gerald M. Edelman, "Through a Computer Darkly: Group Selection and Higher Brain Function," *Academy of Arts and Sciences Bulletin* 36 (October 1982): 38.

[5]José Ortega y Gasset, *The Dehumanization of Art and Other Writings on Art and Culture* (Garden City, N.Y.: Doubleday, n.d.), p. 30.

this delightful figure as being itself something more than a metaphor.

Before we examine the role of metaphor in the dream, we must briefly look at it from the rhetorical perspective. We are beginning to see not only that the master tropes are capable of any combination (ironic metaphors, metaphoric ironies, synecdochic metonymies, and so on), but also that it is difficult to keep one trope separate from the others. Some theories even collapse the number of tropes to three or even two by simply redefining the scope of their operations. Moreover, one might maintain that all four tropes are species of metaphor in that all are displacements of substance within a certain order of resemblance, or that all four are ironies in that they are masquerading as something they are not (trope itself means "turn"). The problem with assigning a figure to a single tropological category (*this* is a metaphor, *this* is a synecdoche) is that one figure may quite freely appropriate, or "trump," the products of another. For example, we recognize the figure "my tongue shall be my steel" as a metaphor that, depending on the context, may mean either "my eloquence shall be my weapon" or "my weapon shall be my eloquence"— eloquence (power, persuasion, etc.) being the point of resemblance. But the metaphor is really made of two signifiers that are already figures in their own right. In fact, we may define "tongue" and "steel" either as metonymies, in the sense that they reduce intangibles (language, power) to tangibles, or as synecdoches, in the sense that they represent parts of wholes. Still another view might argue that "tongue" is a metonymy but that "steel" is a synecdoche, or vice versa. In any event, the overarching, or coupling, strategy is metaphoric, and possibly metaphoric-ironic, in that the speaker seems to be reversing expectations of how success might best be achieved in the situation. In short, we are involved here with the mental operations of reduction, combination, and opposition, and we end up with figures that are made of other figures. So we need to bear in mind that it is the strategy and not the finite image itself that we are trying to trace into the dream-work.

If there is a privileged trope among the master tropes, it is by all odds metaphor, which seems to be ever susceptible, in our modern definitions, to all the abuses of its own acquisitive nature. Jonathan Culler, following Tzvetan Todorov and the Groupe de Liège, suggests that metaphor is a combination of two synecdoches because "it moves from a whole to one of its parts to another whole which contains that part."[6] On the other hand, Albert Henry sees metaphor as "the synthesis of a double metonymy in short circuit."[7] Either view suggests the difference between what I call the metonymic-synecdochic and the metaphoric-ironic processes as they relate to dreams: if metonymies and synecdoches are forms of reduction (like division and substraction), metaphor (along with irony) is a form of expansion (like addition and multiplication)—that is, the operation by which the brain adds one thing to another, getting from one metaphor or metonymy or synecdoche to another.[8] Metaphor is the family-hopping trope, it seeks its

[6]Jonathan Culler, *Structuralist Poetics: Structuralism, Linguistics, and the Study of Literature* (Ithaca, N.Y.: Cornell University Press, 1975), p. 180.

[7]Albert Henry, *Métonymie et métaphore* (Paris: Klincksieck, 1971), p. 66.

[8]In this study I deliberately restrict my application of both metonymy and synecdoche to a one-way operation. According to most definitions, true metonymies and synecdoches may move in a nonreductive, or expansive, direction, though in my experience this is relatively rare. In the case of metonymy, you can go not only from cause to effect but also from effect to cause; in the case of synecdoche, you can go not only from whole to part (reductive) but also from part to whole (expansive). One reason I choose Burke's definitions is that Burke emphasizes the reductive strategies of these tropes. But finally, it is not the trope that interests me as much as how it can help explain the possible strategies of dreams.

relatives in foreign company. "The mind," Richards says, "is a connecting organ, it works only by connecting and it can connect any two things in an indefinitely large number of different ways."[9] One might say the mind is continually and involuntarily on the lookout for metaphors. I look at a massive bank of clouds and, behold, they are galloping horses or monstrous faces. This place reminds me of that place. Sam reminds me of Charles, whom I have not seen in years, and it occurs to me that both of them look like Dwight Eisenhower. The truth is, I do not make these things into these other things; they become them without my permission. And here we have another cryptic evidence of unconscious or nonsensory thought, which projects itself out of me into nature as if it were an outside force. My mind is all around me, and thought is carried forth metaphorically, playfully, as Gadamer might say, in my confrontation with the shapes of experience.

For metaphor we might substitute Freud's principle of displacement, at least to the degree that in both there is a locative shift from one thing to another and a certain carryover of features or attributes.[10] I have suggested that what is required for the advent of a dream is a conversion

[9]I. A. Richards, *The Philosophy of Rhetoric* (London: Oxford University Press, 1976), p. 125.

[10]See Freud, SE 4:307–308. Jacques Lacan, like most psychoanalysts, holds the position precisely opposite mine on this point. The Freudian principle of condensation is "the field of metaphor," and displacement is the field of metonymy; metaphor involves "the superimposition of signifiers," and metonymy is "the main method by which the unconscious gets around censorship" ("The Insistence of the Letter in the Unconscious," *Yale French Studies* 36–37 [1966], 129). See also Jean Laplanche and Serge Leclaire, "The Unconscious: A Psychoanalytic Study," *Yale French Studies* 48 (1972): "Metonymy is precisely the figure that emphasizes the connection between one signifier and another, thus sustaining the whole elementary mechanism of language, which dreams exploit without limit" (p. 150).

similar in kind to the mental act of making a metonymy. I do not speak of using a metonymy in the ready-made sense of "heart" for "love" or "tongue" for "eloquence," but in the sense of an image that is made out of the self's unique life in time. The image becomes a metaphor the instant it enters the dream current. My distinction, then, is that metonymy pertains to the birth of an image and that metaphor pertains to its active life in the dream.

Before I can clarify this idea, we must look at how dream metaphors differ from poetic metaphors. To this end it will be useful to turn to Richards' principles of tenor and vehicle. As one of his examples, Richards cites Denham's lines on the Thames: "O could I flow like thee, and make thy stream / My great exemplar as it is my theme." Here, Richards says, "the flow of the poet's mind . . . is the tenor, and the river the vehicle."[11] Richards tends to think of a metaphor as a two-part structure with a subject, or underlying idea, on one side and the metaphorical figure, or vehicle, on the other. But perhaps it would be more helpful, at least in graphic terms, to think of a metaphor as having, in effect, three parts: two different things, one of which may be implicit, and a resemblance that is categorically different from the things themselves. Thus, in Denham's lines, "mind" and "river" stand in a parallel relation of disparity or nonresemblance, but they are united by the likeness of "flow." My objective is not to correct Richards, whose theory makes sense on its own ground, but to bring out what is different about dream images considered as metaphors. All poetic metaphors have three components: the two terms (or signifiers) of the comparison ("mind" and "river") and a resemblance, or tenor, that is *made of* at least one discernible feature shared by both terms. Even the simplest metaphor (e.g., "my

---

[11]Richards, *Philosophy of Rhetoric*, p. 121.

flame" when I am implicitly referring to my love) is perceptually a tripartite tension, or an oscillation of semantic and pictorial energy in a kind of triangular mental space. Dream images, however, do not have three parts. They are "Richardian" metaphors in that the tenor has collapsed into the vehicle and is lost. It might be found by an analyst or an interpreter, but that has nothing to do with the mode in which the image is experienced. For example, we can easily see that the faucet in the young man's dream is a metaphor for penis, which is implicit, or that the choker is a metaphor for femininity in Emily's dream, but this is possible because the dream is being recalled in the conscious state rather than experienced in the dream state. And even then it is an inference we are making about the meaning of the image. But consider a dream reported by C. Mason Myers in which Myers "thought he was swimming upward from the dark of a lake bottom toward the light of the surface, and that the water was identical with truth, the water near the surface being a higher grade of truth than that near the bottom."[12] Taken literally, as Myers says, this amounts to an absurd confusion of categories, though it is no more absurd than Denham wishing his mind could flow like the Thames. Myers' point is that the dream is metaphorical not only from the waking analytical perspective but from the perspective of the dreamer as well—the dreamer simply does not know he is swimming in a metaphor! But he "implicitly grasps" the fact that his rise to the surface has an "identical" connection with truth. But is it really a matter of grasping at all? Does the dreamer grasp anything, any more than I grasp that I am breathing air and walking on the grass? May we not take the word "identical" quite literally? Dreams are *literal*

[12]C. Mason Myers, "Metaphors and the Intelligibility of Dreams," *Philosophy and Rhetoric* 2 (Spring 1969): 92.

metaphors. To Myers, while he was dreaming, the lake *was* truth, not a metaphor for truth, just as the pipes in my irrigation system *were* the constituent parts of my dream theory and I was completely convinced that when I had arranged them correctly I had solved my dream problem. Gregor Samsa did not think of himself as being *like* "some monstrous kind of vermin," he became one, and if Denham were dreaming his line instead of speaking it, he would have the unique experience of composing a poem as he flowed downstream on the current of his own mind.

In a dream, then, the metaphorical operation loses its entire foundation in resemblance: nothing is *like* anything in a dream, and this is what makes the dream's irresponsibility possible. As Richards says, the very idea of likeness involves an awareness of difference: "Some similarity will commonly be the ostensive ground of the shift, but the peculiar modification of the tenor which the vehicle brings about is even more the work of their unlikenesses than of their likenesses" (p. 127). In reading or hearing a metaphor, then, the likeness is always seen in the framework of the opposition, otherwise the metaphor would collapse into an identity, as it does in a dream. Only awake can we be aware that something is a metaphor. Of course, it is quite possible to make a metaphor while you are dreaming and to know that it is a metaphor. For example, I may be talking to John in a dream and think "John is a fox," meaning that John is being devious or cunning with me. Or I might go to a poetry reading in a dream and hear all sorts of metaphors, knowing they were exactly that. What I cannot do in a dream, however, is say "John is a fox, but it's all right because he is just a figure in my dream anyway." I have no desire here to broach the subject of lucid dreams (or dreams in which we are conscious of dreaming), something I have only vaguely experienced. Perhaps it is possible to dream lucidly, but a fully lucid dream seems to me a contradiction in consciousness states, and I wonder if people who say they are aware that they are dreaming during a dream are not really dreaming they are aware that they are dreaming—otherwise, wouldn't they be awake? (This bears on Malcolm's famous argument about making judgments in sleep and whether one can truly assert a sentence like "I am asleep."[13]) To return to Myers, however, if Myers were suddenly to become lucid during his dream (become cognitively aware that he was in a dream), he would immediately develop a metaphorical "competence" and see that "this lake" *seems* to mean truth because it is deep and leads to enlightenment.

As for the irresponsibility of the dream, suppose I hurl together a truly absurd metaphor that couples some of these poetic themes but does not yet have the context of a poem. Here, let us say, is the first line of a poem that was so bad that it literally killed the poet and we shall never know what he had in mind:

[13]Norman Malcolm, *Dreaming* (New York: Humanities Press, 1959). See also the collection of essays addressing Malcolm's theory: *Philosophical Essays on Dreaming,* ed. Charles E. M. Dunlop (Ithaca, N.Y.: Cornell University Press, 1977). As an example of what I mean about the paradox of lucid dreaming, though hardly a proof of the point, I had a dream in which a long-dead relative took me to the bedside of my father, who was dying. Seeing him, I thought, "But my father is already dead. I must be dreaming. I must observe everything very carefully." I recall feeling elated that I had finally managed to get "inside" a dream with all my waking faculties intact. And when I woke up I remembered everything vividly. The problem is that what I remembered, or brought back, was nothing more than what I typically recall of dreams that are not accompanied by an awareness that I-am-dreaming. I had simply brought into the dream a wish, as Freud would say, that I might retain lucidity during the dream. In short, I was dreaming that I was lucid. It is significant that I was unable to make the same observation about the long-dead relative who was alive in the dream. In other words, my lucidity was selective and therefore not an example of true lucidity.

Metaphor

My love, brash refrigerator on the craven stream!

You would have to try out a lot of tenors before you found one that fit this line, and in the end you would probably have to admit that it is an irresponsible image, unless it simply intends to be funny or parodistic. But let me confess that I am rather pleased with the line and have carefully tried to improve it over several drafts, aiming not to make it more sensible or evocative, but more difficult within a certain context of coherence. Perhaps you can see the refrigerator bobbing down a stream, and perhaps a woman clinging to it or riding on it, though it is difficult to know how the refrigerator is being brash and the stream craven, because the craven image seems to be victimizing the brash one. Or perhaps the stream is behaving in a cowardly way because the refrigerator had brashly entered it. But if you figure that out, what has it all to do with my cold, drowning love? Still, you see, it makes a certain nonsense.

A dream could easily produce such an image because it would have nothing to do with meaning, in the usual sense of the word. It would have to do with a feeling, which as the tenor would arise first and then let itself hitch a ride on the first vehicle that came floating by. We probably pay far too much attention to the *sense* we would like dreams to make. It does not occur to us that dreams are, after all, human with respect to their efficiency. For instance, quite often in the waking state we find ourselves making a mental connection that instantly proves silly or embarrassing (puns, for example, are particularly susceptible to silliness), and there seems to be no reason to assume that the brain could not do the same thing while it dreams. Most dream vehicles are probably responsible in that they have some metaphorical relation to the tenor (as "lake" does to "truth") that we can appreciate on waking. But what sort

137

of a tenor could have brought on my floating refrigerator? Clearly there is something sexual going on, but how can a dream *feel* brash and chilly at the same time? I have no idea. However, as one who has dwelled in dreams among brash refrigerators and craven streams, I can only think that a tenor need not be comprehensible as a semantic unity. Could a tenor not consist of a contradiction or an unresolved conflict between qualitative options ("brash" and "craven")? Could one not arrive at a feeling of balanced opposition or at what William Empson referred to, at the seventh level of ambiguity, as something that is "at once an indecision and a structure"?[14] In other words, there are all sorts of feelings that are not bound by categories for which we have words in the waking world. You *can* have a brash refrigerator in a dream—as you can in poetry, if it is contextually coherent—because brashness, like Myers' truth, is projected onto the image rather than being derived from it. It is a strictly private metaphor, by which I mean that its connotative domains are not shared in our common usage of these terms. There is some question, therefore, about whether it can be called a metaphor at all, properly speaking. For example, Gérard Genette questions whether the images of surrealist writing (e.g., Breton's "cat-headed dew" or Eluard's "the boats of your eyes") can be reduced to purely metaphorical processes.[15] But I am assuming that in the dream image, the dreamer, who is not dreaming for a public audience, carries his or her own personally established set of connotations. The dreamer knows, or rather feels, the "aptness" of the dream image, however publicly nonsensical, just as a waking per-

[14]William Empson, *Seven Types of Ambiguity* (Edinburgh: New Directions, 1949), p. 192. Freud gives an example of a compromised dream in his chapter on "Affects in Dreams," SE 5:468–470.

[15]Gérard Genette, *Figures of Literary Discourse,* trans. Alan Sheridan (New York: Columbia University Press, 1982), p. 118.

son can feel the aptness of "the morn in russet mantle
clad."

One of my underlying assumptions is that there is nothing about *being* that is too insignificant or meaningless to
become an element in a dream, and that anything from the
day-residue, or any other day's residue, might, by virtue
of having gotten into the dream on some neural pretext,
lodge itself in the dream-work and figure as one of its
parts. Most dream images seem to be expressive of the
dream's manifest content. They fit in—which is to say that
awake we can see a logic in their presence. But how do we
know *how* they are fitting in? If we consider the dream as a
process of thought, instead of as a product, then we must
surely grant it a "first draft" status, in which case many of
its metaphors are actually mistakes. Should we not, then,
allow the possibility that there are compromises, warring
priorities, and accidents in the process and that the dream,
having no choice, simply incorporates them into its structure? Such an element might be likened to a grain of sand
fallen into a mollusk; the mollusk will simply work
around it and treat it as an organic accretion, putting it
altogether at home in the mollusk world. Thus, in dreams,
something that may have originated randomly is also
something that belongs. It is the belongingness that is apparent during the dream, the randomness that emerges
when we awake and reflect on the strangeness—for instance, carrying a tennis racket to a funeral ceremony. It is
out of such strangeness that the notion of dream symbolism arises. Such things *must* mean something, and indeed they can always be assigned a meaning on a dozen
different contextual bases: a tennis racket is inappropriate
(disrespect for the dead person?), it is both vaginal and
phallic in shape (what is the sexual status of the carrier? the
corpse?), it is an aggressive-playful instrument, and it
probably has a whole range of connotations in the dream-

er's own life. It may be a relevant dream image on any of these counts, but it may also have popped into the dream because of a slight twinge in the dreamer's "tennis elbow."

But are all these images metaphors? Here we reach the point of overlap between metaphor and metonymy mentioned by Burke, Henry, and others. In the last chapter I called the choker an instance of metonymic reduction, and now I seem to be calling it a metaphor. Moreover, I suspect that Myers' lake is more a metonymy than a true metaphor. Certainly the choker and the lake are primarily metonymies in that they stand for abstractions (femininity and truth) that have in themselves no material basis and no factor of resemblance to their referents. On the other hand, the faucet in the young man's dream is clearly a metaphor (if it is anything) in that it is a penis-equivalent on the basis of a resemblance in shape and emissive capacity. And finally, in the case of my barn dream, we seem to be dealing with neither a metaphor nor a metonymy but something closer to a tautology (how can a barn be *like* another barn?). We must then ask how all these different kinds of images are relevant to a discussion of metaphor in dreams. My major premise here is that it is not the *kind* of image that offers the real instance of metaphor, but the coupling of the image—and it may be a metonymy, a synecdoche, a metaphor, or none of these—with another image. Any sequence of dream images is a metaphorical sequence, but not necessarily a sequence of metaphors—or the things we call metaphors in waking life. I can develop this idea best by beginning with the relationship of the metonymic process to the metaphorical process, and because we are dealing with the nature of imagination itself, we can for the moment lump the poets in with the dreamers. In purely strategic terms, poets and dreamers conceive metonymically but execute metaphorically. If one has a feeling and expresses it in an image, or a system of images, would not the act of expression be a metonymic operation, that is, a tangible equivalent of the feeling? Regarded synecdochically, as Burke would say, the image system would be *representative* of the feeling; regarded metonymically it would be a *reification* of the feeling. It is finally a matter of the perspective from which one views it. But as a ready-made instance of how metonymy and metaphor might cooperate in a text we all know, consider the lines in which we find Hamlet dreaming aloud about his grief:

> O, that this too too sullied flesh would melt,
> Thaw, and resolve itself into a dew.

In comparing his flesh to ice (implicit), Hamlet is making a metaphor. But what brought on the metaphor is the desire for the oblivion of death that condenses itself metonymically into the image. Here the incorporeal, the *wish* to be bodyless, is made corporeal. Richards would say that Hamlet's state of mind is simply the tenor of the metaphor. But treating it strategically, we see that the metaphor is the outcome of a metonymic "resolution." (Indeed, we might define the tenor of any metaphor as a *feeling* that has managed to find a vehicular home.) And the resolution does not cease with the initial reduction. As the soliloquy mounts and its images are compounded and fed back into the metonymic converter of Hamlet's mind, they produce an intensification of the very feeling they would relieve, ending in the impasse (so frequent with Hamlet) of "Break my heart, for I must hold my tongue." Overall, Hamlet's problem is that he is always discharging his feelings (which seem to grow by what they feed on) in inadequate points of focalization (Polonius, Ophelia, Rosencrantz and Guildenstern, etc.) that produce only more emotion and therefore more metaphors.

One might argue that I have confused categories here, that Hamlet's metaphors (sullied flesh, dew, etc.) are proper images but that what I am calling metonymy is simply a motivation for an image. On purely rhetorical grounds, this is true, but from the standpoint of the imagination I am interested only in what operations occur in the birth of images, what we call figures of speech being simply the *results* of certain forms of combination brought on by more-or-less complex feelings. To some degree I am thinking of the metonymic condensation as Genette thinks of Proust's metaphors as being generated by a "metonymic sliding."[16] Genette conceives of metonymy as being based strictly on contiguity (e.g., the nearness of a church to the sea provokes Proust to compare its steeples to tapered fish), but even so it is a meta-figural view of metonymy, and the same principle of the interpenetration of metonymy and metaphor obtains if one takes the view that metonymy involves the reduction of a feeling to an image.

It is essential that we avoid any suggestion that this process is anything like a relay race in which metonymy hands the baton to metaphor, which goes speeding on its own down the track. It is a reciprocal process, a continual interpenetration of feeling and image, and if anything I have simplified it here. But bearing this in mind, we might now move directly to a consideration of my statement that any sequence of dream images is a metaphorical sequence. To begin, a metaphor by Donald Davidson caught my eye: "Metaphor is the dream-work of language."[17] Davidson does not pursue the idea, so I am (as with all metaphors) left on my own. What I think he means is that

[16]Gérard Genette, "Métonymie chez Proust," *Figures III* (Paris: Seuil, 1972), p. 42.

[17]Donald Davidson, "What Metaphors Mean," *Critical Inquiry* 5 (Autumn 1978): 31.

metaphor is similar to the dream in that there is a certain brashness in its way of colonizing the world, annexing new things to it through the casuistry of likeness. If I invert Davidson's idea, I arrive at the other half of its truth: *metaphor is the language of dream-work.* By this I mean not that dreaming is an instrument of communication but that the only way the dreaming brain can process experience for any purpose is to speak of it qualitatively by reconstituting it in new forms. The dream is not primarily a mimetic or representational activity; it is a combinatory one. All experience presumably falls into classes, or if it does not it is the dream's business to put it into classes. And the dream's avoidance of the actual experience of the dreamer is nothing but a preference for the *likeness* in experience that can be determined only, as Richards says, through a shift in vehicle.

This idea can be illustrated by a simple experiment one might perform while waiting to fall asleep. Think of the face of a friend or relative, or of any object. Try to hold it steadily in the mind's eye, as if it were a photograph, and it will escape by turning into something else. The face will produce another face, and another face, and so on. Or the face will give way to a very different sort of image—the bridge of a nose may remind you of a steep hill, your brother's face may remind you of the money he owes you. Altogether the whole evolution will be far more haphazard than any dream you will have. The point is, however, that the brain evolves images whether one is awake or asleep on the fluid basis of likeness; one image always leads to another, and the sequence never follows experience or logic. It taps into various orders of unconnected experience somewhat as a tornado, following its own meteorological logic, skips erratically over the earth, destroying this block, ignoring that one, and so on. But the point is that what we refer to as an image is itself only a construction of thought, something projected from thought. It is simply thought in transit, nothing formed but something forming, never an identity but always a passage, an intersection that only resembles an image of art in that we recall it as something trapped in time and space.

Metaphor then, as I am thinking of it here, is not a species of trope in the company of other tropes, but a thought-operation that alters our perspective, as Burke puts it, "by incongruity" or by "seeing something *in terms of* something else," bringing out "the thisness of a that, or the thatness of a this."[18] It is not, then, something *used* by the dream, but the way of dreaming itself, the means by which the dream makes a that out of a this, and in turn a next out of a now. "Indeed," Burke says, "the metaphor always has about it precisely this revealing of hitherto unsuspected connectives which we may note in the progressions of a dream."[19] And on a broader scale we can add to this Hayden White's metaphorical conception of history, inspired in part by Burke, which as a "perspective by incongruity" "made of history an arena in which new things can be seen to appear, rather than one in which old elements simply rearrange themselves endlessly in a finite set of possible combinations."[20] And so with the history of the individual. What could be the conceivable purpose of reliving an experience precisely as it occurred or as it is remembered to have occurred? Or, to put it another way, would not one expect that the mind that could make such leaps as we have been discussing would insist on leaping as far as possible, becoming thoroughly proficient in its mas-

[18]Kenneth Burke, *A Grammar of Motives and a Rhetoric of Motives* (Cleveland, Ohio: World, 1962), p. 503.

[19]Kenneth Burke, *Permanence and Change: An Anatomy of Purpose* (Berkeley and Los Angeles: University of California Press, 1984), p. 90.

[20]Hayden White, *Metahistory: The Historical Imagination in Nineteenth-Century Europe* (Baltimore: Johns Hopkins University Press, 1973), p. 149.

tery of the operation? A complete application of this idea must await my discussion of irony's contribution to the metaphorical process, but perhaps we can make some preliminary observations here about the primary role of metaphor in the formation of the dream plot. As a movement from one object, event, or thing to another via the path of a resemblance, we may say that metaphor is a *seeking* action, a restlessness born of the inability of the image to remain self-contained. Thus metaphor, this escape from the stasis of identity, is the very momentum of thought.

It is true that there is something metaphorical about metonymy and synecdoche (all figures go somewhere), but they are substantially operations of consolidation, of assigning things their emblems and the signs by which we know them. Thus the metonymic-synecdochic process strives to maintain the feeling under the sign of a tangible whole; the metaphoric-ironic process strives to advance the feeling to new contexts. This is not a warfare but what Burke would call a "cooperative competition," in essence a rhythm, as in Susanne Langer's definition of rhythm as a fusion of sameness and novelty. A dream would be rhythmic in the sense that it was continually producing something novel out of something old. In the realm of poetry, metaphor is a finite construction ("my love, my flame!"), but in a dream it is a step in a plot about "my love" in that in expressing a quality about "my love" I have unleashed it in a certain direction. (Things, so to speak, are heating up.) My flaming love calls, then, for its sequel, a consummation of its energy, a fresh metaphorical leap. This is the "and then . . ." of the dream plot, wherein the dream is an evolution from an implicit to an explicit and from an implicit in that explicit to another implicit. Thus every dream image is bi-temporal; its present is a collusion of past and future in which my attention is trapped between "something is happening that is going to happen" and "something is going to happen to what has just happened."

To some extent, all this is phenomenally true of the film and the theater image as well, not to mention the passage of the world before our eyes. The difference is that the dream is *only* imagery, without objective foundation or material impediment. The dream unfolds its world at the speed of thought, and as we dream we are unaware that everything is continually disappearing and being replaced in kind. We see this most clearly, again, in the faces of our dreams. To return to our Frankenstein principle, the dream has a remarkable ability to create new people out of the parts of other wholes. Most of my dream people are people I do not know, who are "made" in the dream-work. I suspect that they are all remnants of friends, acquaintances, and public figures pieced together from the cemetery of my memory and given life by an emotional charge. But it is also possible that they are composites drawn from my lifetime of faces. For instance, when you say "That man next to us looks like Charles" you are performing a complex act of associational searching. You are recognizing Charles' chin and forehead, or deep-set eyes and high cheekbones, in a "complete" stranger in whom there is just enough Charles tenor to summon the entire face, whereas, had the chin been narrower you might have thought of Charles' brother (who looks something like Charles) or Sam, or no one at all. (And who has not wondered how nature could possibly make so many unique faces on such a little grid of flesh without falling into the duplications of assembly-line production?)

Are not all dream faces unstable composites? In fact, the general law behind this claim might be stated as follows: *all places, people, and objects that appear in dreams are composites.* If nothing else, a recognized object, person, or place is a self-composite, born of an accretion of the dreamer's exposures to it over time. But let us remain with faces, which are by far the more interesting form of dream composites. Which image of Charles is stored in my brain? The young Charles?

the older Charles? the bearded Charles? the Charles who wears glasses? Certainly, as Edelman would insist, Charles is already a composite spread out over many synapses, and there is even some doubt that there is, somewhere along the cortical path, a single image of Charles at all, imprinted at a specific moment in his life. Moreover, what of the Charles look-alikes—are they stored next to my Charles-composite, and do they sometimes contaminate Charles? All this is to say that Charles is probably never himself, or only himself, in my dream, and that the stranger is never only a stranger. They are unstable images from my psychic repertory of faces. In a word, all dream faces are synchronic. For example, I have been reading about Nancy Burson's astonishing photograph entitled *Androgyne* (Figure 1), which

Figure 1. Androgyne

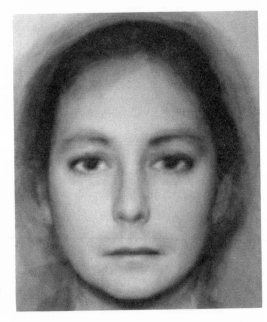

Nancy Burson, with Richard Carling and David Kramlich

is a blend of snapshots of six men and six women fed into a computer programmed to merge facial features.[21] I doubt anyone would know that the photo was a composite by simply glancing at it, but the best word for it is "dream-like." The "person" looks at you out of deep, sad eyes with that oddly generic expression you see in the police sketches of the wanted assailant. It is an intense, *hypothetical* face, and if you saw it on the street it would give you a Proustian sensation of meeting an old acquaintance whose face you couldn't quite pin down. My first thought was that the brain could not do something that subtle, but then I remembered that the brain had invented the computer. But here is a master metaphor for the sort of metaphorical bonding that may be behind all the people and places of our dreams. Known and unknown, it is finally the same process. Each person or place is at once discrete and composite, a many buried in a one. We know this not on any ocular evidence that appears on the face or in the scene, but in our dreamlike complicity with the image. In a word, we are dreaming the image not from memory but from the imagination, some-what as a modern artist strives to put something in the portrait beyond resemblance. But you will say, "Mother appeared to me so vividly! She was just as I remember her in life." But why so vividly? What is behind this vividness—since it did not occur to you that your mother was so vivid in life—unless there has been some psychic tampering with her, a generic perfection of her possibilities that is simply an instantaneous graphic condensation of a history of feeling about her? Dream recall is extratemporal, at least in the sense that it is drawn from a reservoir of likenesses belong-ing to no particular time. The dream image, therefore, is vivid—*when* it is vivid—not because it is sharply detailed, like a drawing or a photograph, but because it is drawn in

[21] See *Harper's*, June 1985, p. 28. This is precisely the effect that Freud discusses in comparing a composite face in one of his dreams with Galton's composite photographs: *SE* 4:139.

neuronal space rather than in a real space inside the head. It is an excitation, not an emanation. Vividness, then, is a certain strength behind the image and not a fidelity of line, shape, form, and so on. It is as if the truth of the image, like all truths, were based on its repeatability. Put another way, your mother has never, unless in another dream, been the vehicle of her own tenor. Now we can see fully that the thought going into the image is only half pictorial and that to have produced an image of such vividness and depth is a matter not of a certain competence of the mind's eye but of the projection of interiorized feeling that transforms what it falls on—much as the feeling of love, falling onto the ordinary face of the beloved, causes it to become a thing of vivid beauty.[22]

And so it is that everything in the dream is not precisely itself. It shimmers with likeness, not only to itself but also to everything it is like. Hence the peculiar depth of the dream image is not simply a spatial depth, but something like the depth of sound that seems to echo spaciously through time. The dream at every moment is a history of one's perception of the world.

[22]There is another approach to the problem of why we see faces imperfectly in dreams. Could our fusion, or con-fusion, of faces have to do with the brain's inability to see a face clearly in the mind's eye? We can all recognize a familiar face when we see it, but can we remake that same face in the imagination? If I conjure the face of my son I get a good general impression and a certain degree of articulation of features. But as soon as I try to look directly at a particular feature, the articulateness I thought was there retreats to another part of the face in my peripheral vision. In other words, everything seems to be there, you just cannot see it. Now, unless our ability to see images eidetically (that is, photographically exactly) is enhanced in the dream state, it is possible that we are simply unable to reproduce the face, much of the time, and hence we produce these amalgamations that mean well but somehow miss being faithful copies. If this is the case, my theory of the metaphorical composite may be seen as suggesting how the dream can make a poetic virtue out of a physiological failing.

6 Irony

W E CAN PAIR metaphor and irony as fraternal strategies, as we have paired metonymy and synecdoche,
because they are both ways of moving beyond single entities. Metaphor is a way of uncovering the likeness of two
different things, irony is a way of uncovering a thing's
extreme potential for not being what it appears to be.
Metaphor says, "This is (like) that"; irony says, "But this
is that!" Both, then, are shocking rather than soothing
tropes in that they produce the surprise of a shift in identity, like that of the comic cognitio. Placed in the company
of irony, metaphor is anything but a stable figure, as metonymy and synecdoche are. Even as metaphor advertises
that it has sought and found unity and compatibility where
"logically" we saw none, it has said in effect, "You see
how unstable our categories are." Thus metaphor and
irony are the binary tropes, they refer us to the duality of
experience and perception, to *trans*actions, concealments,
and disclosures in nature. Ultimately they present us with
a mimesis of the self-other enigma, and this is their greatest power in the dream.

Burke equates irony with dialectic and drama, and we can
see how metaphor itself already leans in this direction.

Every metaphor inherently announces a dialectical world. The concept of resemblance is itself dialectical, for it presumes a concept of difference. The surprise of metaphor is its double triumph over identity and difference, over oneness and two-or-more-ness. The ironic basis of dialectic's thesis-antithesis is that you can never trust the world— or rather you can trust it, more or less, to contradict you. As the dialectician puts it, all categories are unstable because they are imperfect, and this universal instability—this "internal fatality," as Burke puts it, built into the structure of macrocosm and microcosm—"places the essence of drama and dialectic in the irony of the 'peripety,' the strategic moment of reversal."[1] But fundamentally the dialectical habit is something built into the brain as a survival technique—that is, through dialectic we anticipate extreme uncertainties, what *could* happen if the world were perfectly imperfect and produced only perfect contradictions. And in the dream where we are so frequently endangered, we produce dialectical images—or we produce dramas (or, if you will, ironies) that from one point of view at least are the means by which the self musters its enemies and its concerns in the form of a surrogate reality.

Let us see how the metaphoric-ironic process asserts itself in the plots of dreams. How the dream manages the feat of developing even a rudimentary plot is anyone's guess, but a possible theory might run like this: as soon as the dream feeling condenses itself metonymically into an image (perhaps at the point were the EEG begins to pick up REM signals), the image seeks out its destiny as a metaphor, which is to construct a dynamic world motivated by that particular feeling. The most obvious characteristic of the dream is that it is *driven on*. As Bachelard says, it is

[1]Kenneth Burke, *A Grammar of Motives and a Rhetoric of Motives* (Cleveland: World, 1962), p. 517.

151

hungry for images; the image spawns images and thereby the dream takes that course of imaginative movement we call fiction, separating and combining its elements along the axis of a dream plot, which is nothing more than a volume of feeling spending itself in a path of least resistance. With the help of irony this frequently turns out to be the path of maximum intensity.

But most dreams are pedestrian affairs, hardly the stuff of good fiction (putting aside the dream fiction of artists like Kafka and Stevenson). We can see just how "artless" dreams are if we put them against a fairly simple definition of narrative like Tzvetan Todorov's: "the shift from one equilibrium to another . . . , separated by a period of imbalance."[2] Dreams do not proceed on such a structure, partly because they do not (at least narratively) begin and end. A dream seems to be a steady disequilibrium, with no functional or thematic interest in solving or rounding out a problem. The narrative of the dream is concerned with *ramifications* of a tension, or what I earlier referred to as enigma variations—not with getting me into trouble (or pleasure) and out of it, but with extending the trouble (or pleasure) to the boundaries of the feeling that produced the dream. The dream image is simply the "object" on which the feeling falls, like a mist, and at the borders of the feeling there is simply the void of slow-wave sleep. So if I am frustrated, terrified, or lost in one episode, I am likely to remain so in succeeding episodes, until a new master image changes the key of the dream. And even when the key is changed, by waking or by a return to non-REM or slow-wave sleep, there is evidence that subsequent dreams will in

[2]Tzvetan Todorov, "Structural Analysis of Narrative," in *Contemporary Literary Criticism: Modernism through Poststructuralism,* ed. Robert Con Davis (New York: Longman, 1986), p. 328. See also Todorov, *The Fantastic: A Structural Approach to a Literary Genre,* trans. Richard Howard (Ithaca, N.Y.: Cornell University Press, 1980).

some form continue to pursue the same enigma. In general, dreams have a monotonal or stubborn quality that is often felt by the dreamer as an inexplicable entrapment, not always unpleasant, in a world of limited potentiality. Again, as Sartre says, "events occur as if not being able not to happen, in correlation with a consciousness which cannot help imagining them."[3] This returns us to our principle of the "locked revolver," whereby the dreamer vaguely seems to have ordained what has happened. This is not in the nature of a prediction, but a *déjà pensé,* of things coming about as if they had already happened.

What keeps the dream from being dull to the dreamer is the fact that it is perceived not as a fiction but as an experience. But this is only a partial explanation, because experience, as we all know, can be very dull. In the dream, however, the world surrounds us in a peculiar way. Thanks to this fusion of event and consciousness, it is not simply any old world, but one in thrall to a unique physics. This is plainly the perception of the waking mind (to the dreamer everything is quite normal). But in recalling the dream experience, we see that everything seemed to be possessed by an urgency. In a dream things exist at great speed. Even a bored person encountered in a dream appears as animated by boredom, he is vividly bored— which is to say, in the end, that he is an imaginary creature apprehended as a reality (imagine meeting Hamlet in a real hallway!). Like a work of art, he is stripped of excess, the incarnation of a certain feeling, even if he is simply a part of a crowd.

The dreamer's interest in the dream, then, is a function not of "interesting" events but of the fact that the dream observes no periodicities of temporal existence (in which

---

[3]Jean-Paul Sartre, *The Psychology of Imagination,* trans. Bernard Frechtman (New York: Washington Square Press, 1968), p. 220.

real boredom is always embedded) and no contingencies of spatial existence. All that detains us in the real world is absent in the dream. Time and space are nothing more than a field of convenience in which the dream image exploits its possibilities. Imagination, Mary Warnock says, is free, unlike memory, which "is tied to the production of ideas joined as they were, and in the order in which they originally came as impressions." The nature of imagination is "to slide smoothly from like idea to like idea, and to continue in any course once set, producing more and more similar ideas according to the principles of association."[4] We can now see that the Parnassian principle, which operates on every level of the dream, is primarily a metaphorical agency in that it freely mixes experience from different times and places according to a transcendental tenor that is nothing less than the momentary continuity of the dreaming self. As metaphors, dreams have no more respect for empirical categories than birds have for property lines.

But if the dream plot were ruled entirely by the metaphorical impulse, it would probably become as chaotic as a surrealist play as it hopped from one likeness to another likeness to another on the basis of any associational cue. In other words, the metaphorical process in itself does not account for a coherent progression of images, either in fiction or in the relaxed environment of the dream. We tend to take for granted the dream's capacity to develop a story. When we tell our dream to someone, we speak as if the plot had been made up by a ghostwriter. But when you consider that your mind *did* this *while* you experienced it, the most pedestrian dream plot should earn your respect. But at what level does the conception take place? I suggest that it is primarily a metaphorical operation, be-

[4]Mary Warnock, *Imagination* (Berkeley and Los Angeles: University of California Press, 1978), p. 133.

cause metaphor is our clearest instance of the mind's ability to link things together. Some rhetoricians might argue that this mental feat belongs more properly under the aegis of metonymy (in the classical definition), insofar as contiguity and cause and effect are basic plot operations—that is, with these principles you can start with any image and develop it in terms of what is likely to happen to it on the premises. Without discounting this as a factor, however, it appears that metaphor is even more fundamental, especially in the dream, because it is the means by which the mind calls up its own rich repositories of association. Cause and effect belong to the world, but only I can conceive of Fred Potts waiting in an alley on a dark night.

Still, in dreams as in fiction, a metaphor must have a direction in order to be expressive. For instance, if you want to speak of your love you can set out in the direction of warmth (flame) or frigidity (ice) or you can oxymoronically split the difference ("my cold flame"). But where do you go from there? How do you make a praxis out of a likeness? It is perfectly natural in rhetoric to speak of metaphor as the figure that finds the likeness in two different things, but making the metaphor, finding the likeness, requires a capability that participates in the strategies demanded for the making of irony, synecdoche, and metonymy. In other words, you have to find the *right* different things that share a likeness (ideally, things *perfectly* different), and you have to be able to locate a likeness, or a part, of these different things that adequately speaks for their wholes. No doubt the dream, as we have already suggested, has no such strictures as obtain in poetry, but it is plain that dreams have a metaphorical capability. Putting aside feverish or obsessive dreams, nightmares, or problem-solving dreams (all of which cling tenaciously to their themes), dreams do have a sense of responsible linearity.

I am suggesting, then, that processes require other processes. Like the chambers of the heart they participate in each other's work, and to do any kind of thinking, insofar as it relies on figuration, the mind needs all the tropes beating in unison. And the contribution of irony to metaphor, as a fellow-traveling trope, is that it serves as a dialectical compass that points in the direction of maximal difference. That the dream image may not always choose to move to the extreme does not really matter. But as all dialecticians and navigators know, you need a reverse direction, a sort of psychic north-south polarity, to discover your directions, whatever they may be. Irony, if nothing else, is the magnetism of opposition against which the dream plots its azimuth.

I shall deal with irony on two very different levels. The first I call *structural irony* because it belongs to the narrative proper (or *mythos*); the second I call *visionary irony* because it relates to something like *dianoia,* or theme, if one can use such a deliberate word in connection with an involuntary activity. By structural irony I mean either specific moments or episodes that have the character of peripeties, or the overall pattern of the dream's organization. Most characteristically, structural irony takes forms like these: the last bus of the night pulls away just as you reach the station; the destination clearly mapped out by your friend is not there when you arrive; or the vehicle that will speed you away from the oncoming enemy will not start; or your revolver is suddenly locked; or the narrow ledge carrying you above the abyss becomes even narrower; or nature calls and there is no bathroom in sight. In such moments the dream world seems, as Roland Barthes says of the tragic reversal, "ruled by a spite that can always find the negative core of happiness itself."[5] These events are

---

[5]Roland Barthes, *On Racine,* trans. Richard Howard (New York: Performing Arts Journal Publications, 1983), p. 44.

not technically ironies, but they proceed from the same
sort of oppositional thinking that Sophocles, for example,
used in bringing poor Oedipus "home" via the Cithaeron
road. It is not that the ironies are always negative in
dreams (dreams also present us with good luck, success,
and well-being), but that the stakes of disaster are always
higher and dreams tend to put us in problematical situations. Behind such peripeties, then, is not so much an
inherent cynicism in the dream as the spectacle of the
mind's alertness. So fine is the line between thought and
image that "this could happen" is transmitted by the
dream-work as "This is happening!" In the dream the
hypothetical and the real are identical.

But there are much subtler forms of structural irony.
For example, let us examine a dream experienced by D.
M. Johnson and reported in an article on why we forget
dreams:

> I recently had a dream in which I remember getting out of
> my car to open the garage door, and noticing that the head-
> lights were on, although I had been driving in the daytime.
> I opened the garage, and it seemed to be night inside, so
> that the headlights brightly illuminated everything there,
> though it was still daylight outside. Nothing in this account
> (a) is vivid, attractive, frightening or especially interesting.
> (b) None of these images occurred, as far as I remember, in
> other dreams. (c) What I dreamed is strange, apparently
> meaningless, and seems not to be part of any larger pat-
> tern.[6]

There is no way to explain why this dream was remembered, because it is so "apparently meaningless." But its
triviality does not mean it is a trivial dream. Dreams are
more often than not about trivial things (for which we can

[6]D. M. Johnson, "Forgetting Dreams," *Philosophy* 54 (1979): 408.

probably be thankful), but they are never trivial in the sense of being themselves boring. I certainly agree with Johnson that the dream is a dull affair *as a content,* and on that level not worth our time. But as an illustration of the ironic powers of the dream, Johnson's is a jewel of clarity. Here the oppositional faculty of the brain can be seen at close range in a sequence of images virtually unencumbered by a plot. The whole basis of imagination is contained in the dream's act of converting day into night through the metaphoric-ironic manipulation of an image that can probably best be described itself as a metonymy. Based either on a contiguous, a cause-effect, or a tangible-intangible relationship, the headlight metonymically contains, or implies, both day and night, darkness and light. In this case the lights are "incorrectly" turned on during the day. Departing from this suggestion, the dream moves ironically to the opposite; instead of turning off the lights, the dream simply turns on the night, remembering even so that it is still day. The process of reversal might be diagramed like this:

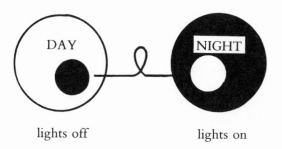

lights off   lights on

The effect is similar to that of a joke, much like the effect of an ironist approaching you in the parking lot and instead of saying "Did you know your headlights were on?" he says, "It *is* very dark today, isn't it?" Or, like Freud's joke about the French marquis who, returning to his chateau and finding the bishop in bed with his wife, walks to the balcony and pronounces a blessing on the world below. In all three cases, the response is absurd yet logical, and this is the basis of irony: to weave a great absurdity with a slender thread of logic.

But there is more than a bad joke in the dream. Reading it, I was immediately reminded of Magritte's painting entitled *The Empire of Light II,* in which we see a dark row of houses partly illuminated by a streetlamp beneath a bright noonday sky. I had coincidentally been reading about Magritte, and the painting in turn reminded me of what Bernard Noel said about it and about Magritte's work in general:

> There is a sequence [in Magritte's method]: contradiction, inspiration, resemblance, which accelerates the mental dynamic. Contradiction is the seizing of two opposing realities having a relation simultaneously contradictory and necessary. . . . Contradiction is the velocity of our logical displacement from One to the Other in the seizing of their identity and of their irremediable difference: they are contraries and they *resemble.* Thought is that seizing which the image expresses by seizing it.[7]

It appears that what occurred in Johnson's dream was an act of seizure that is at once an initiation and an end of thought, an epiphany of thought. Johnson is probably right: the dream has no meaning, in the sense that it semantically refers to something or leads to something. It was an involuntary act of inspiration in which the brain produced a perfect structure—a contradiction that is also a resemblance, either One being the means by which the Other can only be determined. Thus the metaphorical and ironic impulses are perfectly realized in each other. There

[7]Bernard Noel, *Magritte* (New York: Crown, 1977), p. 64.

is nothing ingenious or intelligent about the act of seizure; it belongs to a whole class of verbal devices that includes oxymoron (dark day, bright night), catachresis, punning, and the making of rhymes. Rhyme, in fact, may be defined as the ironic perfection of a random resemblance into a "necessary" difference. "Bright" and "night" is not very interesting as a resemblance in sound until you find a context in which it becomes a resemblance of opposed relations, as in Johnson's dream, Magritte's painting, or Shakespeare's couplet in Sonnet 147:

> For I have sworn thee fair and thought thee bright,
> Who art as black as hell, as dark as night.

Of course, Johnson's dream might turn out to have a meaning beyond all this (a "thing" about forgetting to turn off the headlights, a fear of dark places, etc.). But, like rhyme, the image only enhances meaning. Beneath all possible meanings is the velocity of the displacement, the naked vehicle of enhancement, which is the mind's discovery of the one Other that belongs to the One.

Structural irony is the tendency of the dream to go in what we call full circles rather than in straight or erratic lines. "With the help of irony," Burke says, "developments that led to the rise will, by the further course of their development, 'inevitably' lead to the fall (true irony always, we hold, thus involving an 'internal fatality,' a principle operating from within, though its logic may also be grounded in the nature of the extrinsic scene" (p. 517). By extrinsic scene, for present purposes, we would be referring to the dreamer whose feeling in a particular case would require some form of inevitable or internally fatal development. Dreams rarely get as peripetous as dramas or novels, given the advanced planning required of dramatic works, but they do have a way of catching us in our

160

own traps. In my own case these are normally dreams that culminate in episodes of public embarrassment, often on a theater stage or in the classroom, where I have forgotten either my lines or my lecture notes. These are what we might call tragedies of manners, or trivial tragedies, and having said that much about them, I see no benefit in exposing them to further analysis.

Instead, I would like to examine a more complex example that might stand as a specimen dream (like Freud's Irma dream) because it is convenient for demonstrating the ramifications of a method of interpretation. I chose a personal dream for approximately the same reason as Freud— I know more about the feeling attending the dream (though it was recorded several years ago) and about the relation of the manifest content to the dreamer's own life. And though, as Freud says, "I [may] be met by doubts of the trustworthiness of 'self-analyses' of this kind,"[8] the point of the self-analysis is not to prove something with stacked evidence but to demonstrate a principle of dream behavior that will either be recognizable to my reader or not. In an earlier chapter I spoke about the absurdity (on Freudian grounds) of a dream in which the manifest content would be sexual and the latent content would be non-sexual. I fully believe this to be the case with the following dream. My only regret is that the dream itself could not have been less personal. In any case, in the hope that it will, as Freud said of his Irma dream, "illuminate a problem," here it is:

I am in a narrow bathroom with Mrs. K, the department secretary. We are apparently making a curtain for the window by putting four evenly spaced tacks into the wall, nowhere near the window itself, on a precise horizontal

[8]Freud, *SE* 4:105.

axis. It is not clear why the precision is necessary or what departmental function our work will serve, but she assures me that it is always done this way. I measure the space and put in the last tack, and the bar fits snugly across it. Mrs. K is pleased that I have been so accurate, and I immediately feel a sense of pride in having done the job so well.

The scene fades. I am now in what appears to be a darkly lit livingroom of the same house. The only light, in fact, comes from the bathroom, which is now vacant. It reminds me of the living room in Polanski's *Repulsion,* though this did not occur to me until I woke up. I am talking to R, a colleague, though I recall nothing of what is being said. There is a strange sense of gloom and intimacy in his bearing toward me, and after a time he mutely proposes that we have a homosexual relation. I say nothing. Immediately he goes into a second bathroom, adjoining the first, to have a shower. I return to the first bathroom to urinate. Suddenly I realize with horror that I have virtually consented to a sexual relation with R to be carried out in a moment in the livingroom. My stream strikes the edge of the bowl and splashes on the floor. I wipe it up with toilet paper. The dream ends.

It seems clear enough that the bathroom setting was inspired by my need to "go to the bathroom," which is exactly what I did on waking from the dream. Mrs. K appears in the dream for two reasons: First, that same day I had carried out a small administrative task at her desk involving the number four, about which I was pleased because I am normally very bad about such matters and Mrs. K can be very short and direct with negligent faculty. But second, and more important, my relationship with Mrs. K had recently improved, though it had always been friendly, because I had been encouraging her son, a lapsed student, to finish his degree. In small ways it had become clear that she was grateful for my interest. Somehow, without any overt instances, we had become even more

friendly, as people often do when they have been unex-
pectedly drawn together by a common interest outside of
the professional routine.

The scene with R is much more unpleasant in its implications. There is a clear connection between the dream
and certain events that had taken place in the past few
weeks. Lately, in all my conversations with R, he had
managed to convert the most innocent topic into a criticism of a fellow colleague. His disrespect for this man
seemed so boundless that he took every opportunity to
remark on his ineptitude in a manner that suggested that I
share the opinion. This had become so disturbing that I
began avoiding R's company. I felt guilty, complicitous in
something that was off-limits, and I vowed that on the
next such occasion I would change the subject abruptly or
put a stop to it altogether. I believe this is the basis for the
homosexuality in the dream. It is not homosexuality per
se, but homosexuality as a metaphor for the feeling of
complicity in being drawn into these conversations which
I passively (out of politeness or cowardice in the face of R's
overwhelming personality) did nothing to prevent. In the
dream I did not consent to the relationship, I simply did
nothing to prevent it—precisely the structure of the conversations. Metaphorically, one might say that my col-
legial relationship was homosexual in the sense that it was
a relationship of an intimacy foreign to my sexual preference. The paradigm of it might be the Othello-Iago relationship, which is "homosexual" (and is often played as
such) in that Iago draws Othello into hearing things, per-
mitting things to be said to him, in the very province in
which Othello should have been most protective of his
privacy.

Now let us consider the relationship of the two scenes of
the dream. The first is pleasant or benign, the second is
extremely unpleasant. What are the common denomina-

tors? First, they present two versions of off-limits intimacy. The scene with Mrs. K takes place in a bathroom, a
locale distinctly outside the bounds of our administrative
relationship. But is a bathroom not the logical place for the
scene, given the urinary stimulus together with the recent
closeness between us, the "something out of the routine"
relationship that had been growing over recent weeks?
The bathroom is even narrow and the quarters close. What
I suggest is that the bathroom is a metonymic condensation inspired by a body-feeling. But dreams do not simply
produce empty bathrooms, they put dream-events in
them. Thus the complementary part of the dream feeling
has to do with the scene of intimacy to be played out there,
based on the "four" incident of the same day. It is impossible to know which feeling produced the other, but it seems
clear that the dream knew what it was doing in providing a
place conducive to both designs.

As for the second scene, with R, it appears that my
dream was amplifying a structural resemblance in two social processes taking place in my life at that time. Thus far
the dream is more or less purely metaphorical. But the
progression from one scene to the other introduces an oppositional element in that a benign form of off-limits intimacy is sharply replaced by an unpleasant one. In short,
the metaphor is ironically motivated. We might see
"bathroom," as scene, as semantically containing at least
two features that overlap on different connotations: it is
the "private" room in which one attends to personal
hygiene, and it is a place where the sexual "privates" are
notably in evidence. These two *almost* synonymous features are antonymically distributed between the two
scenes. Because there is no emotional evidence of sexual
desire in the scene with Mrs. K, I can only assume that the
bathroom is primarily nonsexual in its reference. It pertains to privacy rather than to privates. In the scene with

R, this is not the case. Abruptly, the dream reverses the stakes of intimacy, finds its extreme potential, and without altering its structure converts the latently sexual feature of the first scene into the manifest sexuality of the second.

Could it be purely accidental that the scene with Mrs. K preceded the scene with R? Could it as well have been the other way around? That is, is the escalation of the psychic investment the result of a dream logic whereby developments in one scene, by the further course of their development, led "inevitably" to those of the next? This is unprovable either way, but everything about dream structure suggests that there is a principle operating "within" wherein things continue to get "more so" rather than less so. Everything we know about processes suggests that they are rhythmic rather than random constructions, or that the random, if and when it appears in a dream, is somehow made rhythmical. In any event, the bathroom dream seems to be driven by the ironic impulse.

There are other ways of reading the dream, equally ironic in their own way. A psychoanalytic reading might insist that sex *was* at the bottom of it all, that I secretly desired a sexual relationship with Mrs. K, if not with her son, but that—here in this womb of intimacy—she offered me only administrative busywork, in which case the insertion of the four tacks becomes a sexual displacement. In the scene with R, then, I am either punished or rewarded (depending on your bent) by release from an unexpected source, in which case the return to the bathroom in the denouement scene becomes more than a urinary release. A Freudian would probably say that the sexual affect of the dream had undergone a suppression in the dream-work or had been turned into its opposite,[9] and that what I *thought* I felt about R or Mrs. K (or even about her son) is

[9] See Freud, "Affects in Dreams," *SE* 5:460–487.

not proof of anything: the dream may have done a splendid job of disguising the affect from the dreamer because it is simply unacceptable.

Any answer to this argument can only turn on the crucial difference between the expressive and repressive theories of dreaming. My view is that if we assume that even affects are untrustworthy in dreams, the kernel of whatever truth they may contain can be placed under almost any shell. If one maintains that an affect can be suppressed or turned (through the censor) into its opposite, then the dream itself is not only a rebus but a complete construction of the analyst who interprets it—that is, a puzzle with as many solutions as there are analysts. My dream is no longer my own, but an elaborate lie I tell myself because I cannot bear the truth, or at least bear it and sleep through it. There are cases in which a dream affect may not coincide with what we would expect in the waking state. For example, I may feel indifferent to a violent dream-event or pleased by something I might normally fear (e.g., my snake dream). But as Freud has demonstrated in the case of a "disgusting" fecal dream, an unusual affect might be a compromise of conflicting feelings.[10] Determining this, however, is a matter of moving from the affect to its possible constituents in the dream content, or to what Freud calls "the context" (p. 471). Tropologically, the analysis of a dream would proceed from tenor to vehicle(s), it would differ from most psychoanalyses only in the sense that it assumes an expressive honesty in the dream content, regardless of its emotional volatility. The dream is equivalent to its feeling, however unorthodox the associations. Thus, what Freud would call a "screen memory"—an indifferent memory substituted for a repressed one[11]—I

[10]Freud, *SE* 5:468–470.
[11]Freud, "The Psychopathology of Everyday Life," *SE* 6:43–52.

would call a metaphorical deposit—a composite image that may preserve a nest of tenors, of associated feelings, or what in a nonpathological sense we might refer to as a syndrome. The image does not disguise a primal experience, it passes it along as an affective composite that carries, one might say, a neuronal history of that affect. Let me illustrate the idea with an example from Freud's own dream life. The following dream is addressed, Freud believed, to the "feelings of being inhibited, or being glued to the spot, of not being able to get something done . . . , which occur so often in dreams and are so closely akin to feelings of anxiety":

> I was very incompletely dressed and was going upstairs from a flat on the ground floor to a higher storey. I was going up three steps at a time and was delighted at my agility. Suddenly I saw a maid-servant coming down the stairs—coming towards me, that is. I felt ashamed and tried to hurry, and at this point the feeling of being inhibited set in: I was glued to the steps and unable to budge from the spot.[12]

The staircase is a strong sexual symbol for Freud, and when it occurs in the dreams of his patients he almost invariably interprets it as such.[13] In this case, however, it had for Freud no such meaning, or almost none: "The feeling of shame at not being completely dressed is no doubt of a sexual nature; but the maid-servant whom I dreamt about was older than I am, surly and far from attractive."[14] The obvious questions are: Can we trust this? Is Freud suppressing his own suppression? What is the evidential status of his description of the maid (approx-

---

[12]Freud, *SE* 4:238.
[13]Freud, *SE* 5:355n.
[14]Freud, *SE* 4:239.

imately a description of Mrs. K, incidentally)? How might Freud have interpreted this dream had it been reported by a male patient who believed that it was concerned with anxieties about his business life?

I am not interested in turning Freud's own theory of symbolism against his interpretation of the staircase dream. As any student of Freud's dreams will already know, the true etiology of the dream is complexly sexual. Within ten pages Freud returns to the dream, tells us it was "one of a series" and "equally a dream of [sexual] exhibiting" (p. 247). But how does he know this unless he felt it? Freud does not explore this theme any further, but there is some reason to believe that the dream is a censored version of one Freud reported to Fliess in a latter of May 31, 1897, during the period of his self-analysis:

> I dreamed that I was going up a staircase with very few clothes on. I was moving, as the dream explicitly emphasized, with great agility. (My heart—reassurance!) Suddenly I noticed, however, that a woman was coming after me, and thereupon set in the sensation, so common in dreams, of being glued to the spot, of being paralyzed. The accompanying feeling was not anxiety but erotic excitement. So you see how the sensation of paralysis characteristic of sleep was used for the fulfillment of an exhibitionistic wish. Earlier that night I had in fact gone up the stairs from our ground-floor apartment—without a collar, at any rate—and had thought one of our neighbors might be on the stairs.[15]

This might be a different dream in the same series, but it is unlikely. Knowing what we do about Freud's reticence where his private life was concerned and his habit of "editing" his dreams for publication, often with Fliess' help,

---

[15] *The Complete Letters of Sigmund Freud to Wilhelm Fliess, 1887–1904,* trans. and ed. Jeffrey M. Masson (Cambridge, Mass.: Harvard University Press, 1985), p. 249.

this is probably the unexpurgated version of the dream that appears in *The Interpretation of Dreams* (minus the "erotic excitement"), or at least we must assume that Freud was well aware of the sexual overlap in the two dreams. In either case, Freud draws a clear connection between the dream affect and its content. It does not occur to him, in recording either dream, that affect is anything more than a true indicator of the dream's significance, though in one case he consciously softened the affect in the interest of sexual privacy.

But now we reach the point of metaphorical deposit, which brings us to the identity of the old woman on the staircase. In October 1897 Freud wrote to Fliess about his apparently earliest "teacher in sexual matters," "an ugly, elderly but clever woman" about whom Freud had been having disturbing dreams relating to his "impotence as a therapist."[16] In fact, Freud traces her back from the maid-servant in the staircase dream (who is herself a composite of two real servant-women in Freud's immediate life) to an elderly nurse who lived in the household when he was two-and-a-half. It is unclear what sexual role the nurse may have played in Freud's life, but it is through a further association of her with his mother that Freud confessed to Fliess his sexual preoccupation with his mother during that period, and in a letter to Fliess on October 15 he introduces his idea of the Oedipus complex for the first time. None of this volatile material appears in *The Interpretation of Dreams* or in *Psychopathology in Everyday Life,* where the nurse is mentioned again in connection with Freud's hysterical re-action to his mother's temporary absence.[17] The two in-terpretive texts run along together, one for the public car-

---

[16]*Ibid.*, p. 269.

[17]Freud, *SE* 6:49–51. The standard work on the relevance of the staircase dream to Freud's conception of the Oedipus complex is Jim Swan, "*Mater* and Nannie: Freud's Two Mothers and the Discovery of the Oedipus Complex," *American Imago* 31 (Spring 1974): 1–64.

rying the themes of inhibition, personal uncleanliness, shame, and anxiety, the other for Fliess and Freud's own self-analysis carrying the themes of professional impotence, erotic excitement, and Oedipal impulses.

What interests me here is not Freud's understandable censorship of this intimate material, which was none of his public's business, but the route of his "archeology" in tracing the staircase woman back into the prehistory of his childhood. Freud pieces her together out of the "strangest disguises,"[18] out of memory, dreams, and family accounts, and in the end he even confuses as biographical fact details he had apparently invented in a dream.[19] It is one of Freud's most fascinating chapters. But one is led to ask whether this material was repressed or simply forgotten, or how Freud knew, beyond his commitment to his theory, that it had been repressed. Certainly if there were no such phenomenon as repression he would have applied the same process of decoding the image by seeking its affective origins among the forgotten, fused, and confused ruins of his past. Why then repression? Does the objectionableness of the material guarantee its repression? If it can be recovered by conscious archeology, then why should it be disguised by the dream? If bearable in the science of the day, why unbearable in the art of the night? Finally, what impresses one is that the "repressed" can be found in the image, which it haunts. But is its preservation a function of "screening" or of metaphorical density? I return to this subject in my final chapter. Here it suffices to say that

[18]*Complete Letters,* p. 269. See also the staircase dream in *SE* 5:369–370.

[19]In an October 4 letter to Fliess, Freud says he dreamed that the nurse made him steal coins for her (*Complete Letters,* p. 269), but in *Psychopathology of Everyday Life* he claims that "she used to insist on my dutifully handing over to her the small coins I received as presents" (*SE* 6:50).

Freud's term "archeology" seems suggestive in its implication that the archeologist is one who uncovers the lost-in-time, not the hidden-from-the-present. Like Jung's history house of the soul, the mind is continually building itself on its old foundations, taking on their strength while obscuring them with fresh psychic deposits, thus allowing Freud, among thousands of his other projects, to find his old nurse—this thief-seductress-educator obscurely associated with his mother—beneath the maid-servant and concierge who were continually scolding him for spitting on the staircase. "And thus the maid-servant," Freud concludes his analysis, "since she had undertaken the job of carrying on this educational work, acquired the right to be treated in my dream as a reincarnation of the prehistoric old nurse. It is reasonable to suppose that the child loved the old woman who taught him these lessons, in spite of her rough treatment of him."[20]

What I chiefly wanted to show through Freud's dream is a sense of the dream's self-determination: we dream like what we feel like. Freud's multiple interpretation of his staircase dream (or dreams) seems consciously aimed at neutralizing its sexual content for public consumption (and my own dream is obviously open to the same charge). I do not mean that Freud, or anyone else, is necessarily right about his dreams, but simply that the dream expresses its affect directly as a synchronic image poised on the summit of a history, often a history with a paradoxical character. What seems clear in Freud's diachronic recovery of his old nurse is that the links between the images are invariably metaphorical, circulating around a complex nest of feelings of shame, uncleanliness, exhibition and inhibition, mother-love, and a certain degree of nostalgia. This syndrome is the Ariadne thread that runs through the series

[20]Freud, *SE* 4:248.

and that if traced to sufficient length, if such a thing were possible, would doubtless pass through all the corridors of Freud's psychic history. In any case, the whole transaction is a perfect instance of oneiric Darwinism which, like metaphor, is precisely an ongoing revision or "reincarnation" of a persistent pattern in new materials.

I have not submitted my own dream to a full diachronic analysis, but it probably has one, if memory could find it out. The case for my interpretation rests finally on affective grounds, and on this basis I conclude that it is not primarily sexual in character. I submit that sex, however powerful the drive, however much it dominates our lives in extremely basic ways, may itself serve as a metaphorical vehicle for other feelings. As Paul Ricoeur puts it in his discussion of Ernest Jones' theory of symbolism, sexual symbols may be the signifier rather than the signified.[21] Sex can be a modifying adjective rather than a substantive. Just as we can speak metaphorically of the death of an evening or the birth of a business relationship, so we can speak of the sexuality of a nonsexual anxiety or frustration without getting erotic about it. The vocabulary of sex offers a rich fund of structural likenesses, as when we speak unerotically of electrical connections as being either "male" or "female" or of having a flirtation with real estate or of being violated by the Internal Revenue Service. One might argue, "Ah yes, but sex was on your mind when you chose the metaphor." Precisely, but that is rather like saying that agriculture was on the poet's mind when he spoke of his hero plowing the furrows of his love. In other words, if something is said to be *like* sex or *like* farming, it may have to do with the elucidation of a structure or a feeling that is common to two different domains

[21]Paul Ricoeur, *Freud and Philosophy: An Essay on Interpretation,* trans. Denis Savage (New Haven: Yale University Press, 1972), p. 504n.

of "potency"—potency itself being a fundamental word that covers everything from poison to virility. In brief, you can speak or dream about sex without feeling desire, and about farming without wanting to till the soil.

I am sure some psychoanalysts would call my attention to what is undoubtedly a fundamental tenet of psycho-analysis, that everything springs from sexuality. For instance, Nicholas Abraham tells us that everything "is always and necessarily connected with Sex inasmuch as [it] governs the interiority of nucleic life. The pansexualism of Freud . . . means simply that . . . in the body proper, including the genitals, in what is experienced and in fantasy, and extending even to what is called the external world and to others, there is nothing which would not have a constitutive relation to Sex as the universal requirement and origin of all phenomena. Of course, nucleic Sex has nothing to do with the difference between the sexes."[22] To this I must plead guilty, not only for the bathroom dream but for all my other dreams as well. Certainly it makes sense to say that sexuality, on the nucleic level, is at the bottom of all human behavior, though I am not sure how this differs from saying that everything we do or are we owe to the fact of being alive, life being a constant co-habitation of cells. But can we say that our conscious un-awareness of this basic sexuality constitutes a repression, any more, for example, than that our conscious un-awareness of our molecular foundation constitutes a re-pression of our physiology? Is there anything that is *not* a repression? And if there is, on what cognitive grounds could one possibly know?

Still, one might legitimately ask why my bathroom dream was not as literal as Freud's staircase dream in its

[22]Nicholas Abraham, "The Shell and the Kernel," *Diacritics* 9 (Spring 1979): 22.

depiction of its materials. Why was it so devious in carrying office and hallway conversations into the bathroom, if
sex was not latently the real issue? We find the best answer
in the nature of metaphor itself. If you trace intimacy to its
extreme form, you arrive at the sexual sphere. All human
relationships are potentially sexual, just as they are potentially violent, gentle, boring, and so on. But this is not the
same thing as saying that I secretly desire Mrs. K. It means
simply that sexual and other kinds of intimacy are on the
same continuum of likeness, and it is only the continuum
of likeness that interests the mind in the metaphorical
mode. Yet metaphor, with the help of irony, involves
something like the mystical principle of perfection. The
so-called censorship principle is nothing more than the
mind's metaphorical attempt to get out of identity into
likeness and extremity, to an absolute form that might
include all possibles. For instance, imagine the originator
of the Oedipus story (if it had one) beginning with the idea
of a man who kills his uncle and marries his aunt. Before
long it occurs to him that his story is imperfect. It has not
set the stakes high enough, and so in a single leap of imagination he sharpens it to its now famous and definitive
form. In that leap he has imagined the worst of all worst
worsts, in a sense protecting his story against irony by
letting irony be his guide. On the one hand, this ironic leap
would be motivated by the need for sociopsychological
perfection (the incest and patricidal taboos), but on the
other hand the motive would be formal perfection itself—
that is, what we would today call the worst-case scenario,
or the need to go all the way, no matter what the case, on
the intuition that everything potentially contains a final or
absolute form. Much in Ricoeur's commentary on Freudian symbolism runs counter to my thesis here, but I am
congenial to his idea of symbol (or, in my term, image) as
prophecy. Symbols, he says, "carry two vectors": "On

the one hand, symbols repeat our childhood in all the senses, chronological and nonchronological, of that childhood. On the other hand, they explore our adult life." They "represent the projection of our human possibilities onto the area of imagination . . . ; remembrance gives rise to anticipation; archaism gives rise to prophesy"[23] That is, the symbol, or image, is a projection of future possibilities; the past is recomposed as an equation for the cares of the future. In Burkean terms, built into the dialectical psyche is the need to posit the absolute as a means of covering all bases. The creative fiction of the dream is inevitably a wariness toward reality built out of the examples of the past and directed toward future variations. Far from suppressing, the dream confronts the tensions suspended in the feeling. But it confronts them as forms, or potentialities, rather than as identities and desires. There is no point in preparing to meet yesterday's enemy.

The metaphoric-ironic process, then, is the only means by which thought can escape the deadly gravity of sameness. One image metaphorically calls forth another that is *like* it but different. But the dream does not say, this image is like that one; rather, it says that this feeling-structure is like that one, thereby achieving an integration of experience, if that is finally what dreams are doing for us. What is being integrated, one suspects, is not simply present and past experience but a conversion of experience into a "law of feeling." Arthur Koestler suggests that "a too explicit and detailed exposition of the bisociated image has the . . . disadvantage of limiting the validity of the comparison to the author's subjective experience."[24] He is referring to the poetic image, but the same principle can be

---

[23]Ricoeur, *Freud and Philosophy,* pp. 496–497.

[24]Arthur Koestler, *Insight and Outlook: An Inquiry into the Common Foundations of Science, Art, and Social Ethics* (London: Macmillan, 1949), p. 318.

applied to the dream image—that is, a too explicit image, a direct copy of experience stored in the brain without a tropological conversion, would be virtually useless, except to the memory function, because it would always be only itself. It would possess no motility. The brain would then be a storehouse of rigid, isolated memories, or things that had no usefulness in making adjustments to the continually shifting and continually repeating demands of life. Art, among other things, would be impossible. The brain would be like a library in which the books were stacked indiscriminately on the basis of date of acquisition. In order to be fully useful, experience must be filed not only as a memory but also as a metaphor. This is the card-catalog system of the self's history in time, and one can only assume that it operates automatically, involuntarily, and continuously and that at night, owing to the peculiar state of relaxed diligence called sleep, when the brain has full access to its holdings, it takes the character of a dream.

Much of what I want to say about irony as a vision is implicit in the foregoing discussion. Not all dreams are as Aristotelian in structure as the ones I have been examining. Indeed, dreams tend toward a flat syndetic construction similar to the sequence of sideshow events in a carnival or to the stations of a medieval passion cycle (to place the dream somewhere between the grotesque and the sublime). But in any dream construction the irony of lurking reversals is simply a synecdochic part of a larger ironic force that holds sway over the dream. Here we are far above the structural into what we can only call the visionary, and it is best described by Kierkegaard:

> Irony is a determination of subjectivity. With irony the subject is negatively free. The actuality which shall give him content [does not exist], hence he is free from the restraint in which the given actuality binds him, yet nega-

tively free and as such hovering, because there [is nothing] which binds him. It is this very freedom, this hovering, which gives the ironist a certain enthusiasm, for he becomes intoxicated as it were by the infinity of possibles; and should he require consolation for all that has passed away, then let him take refuge in the enormous reserves of the possible. But he does not surrender himself to this enthusiasm; on the contrary, it merely inspires and nourishes the enthusiasm for destruction already within him.[25]

Although Kierkegaard does not intend this to pertain to the dream, it is an almost unimprovable description of the dream's boundless freedom to extend the self into every part of the dreamed world. Here sleep would be conceived of as the liberator from actuality, in the absence of which the dreamer hovers intoxicated over his entire history. The dream, then, is our "consolation for all that has passed away"; it is the personal means by which the individual, as Kierkegaard elsewhere observes of irony, "emancipates himself from the constraint imposed upon him by the continuity of life" (pp. 272–273). Thus the dream is the only state of consciousness in which *being* can survey itself precisely free of repression, for only in the daily world of manners and musts do we repress. In dreams, idolatry of self is canceled in one dream and affirmed in the next. In dreams we may be punished for the day's or for life's hubris, or granted our pleasant vices. The dream giveth and it taketh away. It is of no matter, because the dream, beyond the continuity of the world, is *sans souci,* it simply defines our affair with actuality in a spirit of ironic freeplay.

Thus conceived, irony is what leads metaphor, the im-

---

[25]Søren Kierkegaard, *The Concept of Irony: With Constant Reference to Socrates,* trans. Lee M. Capel (Bloomington: Indiana University Press, 1965), p. 279.

age maker, through the wilderness of resemblances to its embodiment of the self-other enigma. Irony, in itself, is unable to produce the dream, for among the master tropes it is unique in being nonpictorial. Irony is not a way of *seeing as,* but it is a way of seeing *through* or *beyond.* It does not make images, it supervises their fate. It is to metaphor what Iago is to Othello—the goad that compels the dreaming hero, as Kierkegaard says, "to poetically produce himself."[26] Through irony the self deploys its subjectivity into metaphors that have all the appearance of being the objective "others" of the world but are really only the self displaying itself in unrecognizable forms. Like Narcissus, the dreamer gazes into the pool and sees there a horde of stranger-selves, or what in the occult are called "familiars." Unlike Narcissus, however, he feels a dim collusion between himself and the image. But like one's own consciousness it is substantially beneath the grasp, for only occasionally does the dream even hint that it is itself the dreamer. Among literary images, none is more dreamlike in this sense than that moment in *Death in Venice* in the dining room of the hotel when young Tadzio "chanced to turn" and his "strange twilit grey eyes" meet Aschenbach's for the first time. "Chanced to turn"—an event that hovers between the ordinary and the ordained; for is not

[26]In *Actual Minds, Possible Worlds* (Cambridge, Mass.: Harvard University Press, 1986), Jerome Bruner suggests that Milton's Satan "is comparable in its metaphoric power to Freud's Id metaphor of Unreason" (p. 49). To this I would add that both are ironists, at least to the extent that they are "against faith" (p. 50). Of course Freud's Id, like Milton's Satan, has its own "unreasonable" faith, whereas true irony has neither plan nor program unless it is the consternation of all other programs. Irony is what comes running the moment a certainty is proclaimed. But as I understand the Id, it could be said to be up to just this as far as the Superego's plan for the Ego is concerned. Still, insofar as the Id is finitely (i.e., desirously) motivated, it would be relativistic, and (as Burke says, *Grammar,* p. 512) "in relativism there is no irony."

178

the point of the image exactly that the boy is Aschenbach's own imagination seen at a distance? And soon Aschenbach lapses into a reverie in which he ponders "the mysterious harmony" that must exist between the individual form and the universal law, and he concludes that it was all like "the flattering inventions of a dream, which to the waking sense proves worthless and insubstantial."[27]

This is the split mode of the dream, in which the dreamer is both the spectator and the maker of the image and the dream world is only his thought flung out into its shapes and forms. The unique ontology of the dream is that every event is accompanied by its own inevitability, and as a result of this peculiar overlay of destiny the event seems to have its own psychic life, to be permeated with the dreamer's consciousness. It comes down to a single pervasive effect: I have made the dream, but I cannot possess it, for the dream comes *from* me as if it were coming *to* me. Freud speaks of the tendency of dreams to combine "contraries into a unity or [to represent] them as one and the same thing."[28] The contraries I refer to here, however, are contraries not of meaning but of substance, beneath all interpretation or referral to a personal neurosis. To the sensitive dreamer, the self-otherness of the dream is faintly detectable in the images themselves: in the look in the eye of the dream-character, in the slightly intimate attention he pays me, even as he ignores or rejects me—overall, in

---

[27]Thomas Mann, *Death in Venice and Seven Other Stories,* trans. H. T. Lowe-Porter (New York: Random House, 1963), pp. 27–28. It persistently occurs to Aschenbach that his experience in Venice seems to have been shaped "by the fantastic logic that governs our dreams," and, indeed, Mann's own creative logic recalls a characteristic of dreams that I have already discussed: the dream image is always composite. Aschenbach dreams Tadzio, Tadzio is Aschenbach, he is the Spinario, he is Phaedrus and Dionysus, he is death and he is the birth of form.

[28]Freud, *SE* 4:318.

the dream's efficiency in seeing that I am always near its center. Dream people are there *for* me, though far less ostentatiously than the stage actor is there for me. They allow nothing to pass unnoticed. Even the strangers seem to know me; they wear the same looks of complicitous indifference that one sees in the faces on Munch's streets or in the gallery of Kafka's court.

The problem in dealing with all these processes separately is that one falsifies the nature of what happens in the brain in the dream state. I have been trying to describe something that is beneath and prior to language, something that must certainly occur as an involuntary and instantaneous process. I assume only that the creation of dream images would entail, as Freud was the first to suggest, such combinatory patterns of thought as reduction and extension, integration and negation. There is, for example, no assumption that the dream is ever ironic in the conventional definition of that much abused word. But irony, in that sense, is (like metonymy, metaphor, and synecdoche) simply a rhetorical strategy based on the still more elementary mental operation we might characterize as *finding the negative* of something. So the master tropes, as I have conceived them here, are the primary processes of imaginative production and do not occur as separate phenomena. As Burke says, "Give a man but one of them, tell him to exploit its possibilities, and if he is thorough in doing so, he will come upon the other three"[29]—or, in oneiric terms, isolate any moment in a dream, trace its mental origins thoroughly, and you will come upon the operations I have described here from a tropological perspective.[30] Indeed, if we were to carry our notion of the

[29]Burke, *Grammar of Motives,* p. 503.

[30]One might also break the metonymic-synecdochic / metaphoric-ironic pairing down further into the two classic principles of description and narration. The aim of description, as Genette says, is "to represent

tropological operations beyond the realm of the strategic to the realm of realms over which they preside, treating them as a kind of pantheon of muses governing imaginative activity, we might supplement Burke's chart according to the following division of labor:

metonymy = reification
synecdoche = coherence (wholeness)
metaphor = progression
irony = thoroughness

These would be the four "powers" of thought through which imagination produces and develops its images of experience. Metonymy is the reifying power, or the force that brings the image out of the thematic world of feeling and idea into form. It is the first-stage operation, and it is analogous to Nietzsche's plastic Apollonian principle, associated by Nietzsche with the "dream world of the

---

objects simply and solely in their spatial existence, outside of any event and even outside any temporal dimension" (*Figures of Literary Discourse,* trans. Alan Sheridan [New York: Columbia University Press, 1982], p. 133). The fresh image, then, would be an instantaneous description, metonymically established and carrying with it its sum of parts. Narration is concerned with temporal and spatial change in the object/image, the story told by the image. And here the metaphoric-ironic movement would be the primary force. To say "this is like that" is to create a kind of event in which a potential of the image is brought to pass. If the principle of narration is the Heraclitan "everything flows," that of metaphor and irony is "everything becomes its other." The ironic characteristic of metaphor in the dream is that it is a process that does not cease. If in a dream Sarah should remind me of Jane, Jane appears in Sarah, and there is no telling who will survive the collision and lead it in what direction within the drive of the feeling. The dream narrative would be the chronology of the image in all its vicissitudes. See also, in this vein, Peter Brooks, "Freud's Masterplot," *Yale French Studies* 55–56 (1977): 280–300, reprinted in *Reading for the Plot: Design and Intention in Narrative* (New York: Random House, 1985), pp. 90–112.

scene" in which the Dionysiac knowledge, that essential movement of the will in which Nietzsche sees the spirit of music, "again and again discharges itself."[31]

The synecdochic, as I have treated it here, is not simply a sail-for-ship substitution. The idea underlying synecdoche is *relationship:* the part implies or carries with it the whole, or to move centripetally, the whole consists of parts. The act of using the part to represent the whole is not simply a symbolic substitution, but also an expression of wholeness that is an awareness of structuration or coherence. On this level the most exemplary synecdoche would be the part-for-whole relationship, primarily because the use of the whole for the part does not imply relationship. I am not denying that there are whole-for-part synecdoches, but only maintaining that in its ideal form the synecdochic movement involves a controlled mental expansion wherein the very perception that something is *a part* (of something) involves a circumscription, or a framing of a coherence.

Metaphor is the spirit of movement, or progression, from one image to another. Here I am emphasizing not likeness or resemblance but the drive of the figuring mind to find likeness. The urge to make metaphors is really a refinement of a basic fact of perception, that things are perceived both as themselves and as members of a class, that every movement of mind is a relevant movement rather than a random one, a leap based on attraction.

On first glance, the difference between irony's thoroughness and synecdoche's coherence may seem obscure. What I mean is that the business of synecdoche is to see that all parts are, as Burke says, "consubstantially relat-

---

[31]Friedrich Wilhelm Nietzsche, *The Birth of Tragedy and The Genealogy of Morals,* trans. Francis Golffing (Garden City, N.Y.: Doubleday, 1956), p. 56.

ed" (p. 508) to the whole. One might say that synecdoche is imagination's editor, it ensures that all images belong to the same whole. But thoroughness involves another, related operation beyond wholeness. It is the work of irony to ensure that the whole includes all ramifications of the subject. It is one thing to have a unified whole, another to have a whole that has aggressively and dialectically carried its nature and quality as far as possible. Still, there is a competitive affinity in the two operations. Irony is disintegrative in that it is a strategy for avoiding boundaries and final positions. On its own, without grounding in a finite content, it would succumb to the rapture of the infinite and would end up being "about" nothing but further irony (which may be what happens in those haywire dreams of feverish people that seem to go everywhere and nowhere). But in the rigorous self-portraiture of the dream-work, the ironic impulse must be contained within the design of the whole. So, like the charioteer in Plato's *Phaedrus,* where desire and rhetoric are so curiously teamed, it is synecdoche that restrains the license of the unruly dark horse and harnesses its wanton energy to the task of expressing only the "possibles" of the dreaming self.

7 *Rhetoric and Repression*

IT SEEMS APPROPRIATE to close by drawing some final distinctions between repression and expression, insofar as these are behavioral acts that can be observed taking place rhetorically. To this end, we shift our attention from the dream to literary texts. The consequence should be minimal, because the imagination that dreams is the same imagination that produces waking fictions. But the major problem in using a dream, or commentary on dreams, as a subject for analysis of this sort is that the dream cannot be interpreted, as either expression, repression, or anything else, without an exhaustive examination of its context in the dreamer's psychic life. As we have seen, a dream's meaning, or significance is always outside its "text," unlike the possible meanings of a literary text that are available, comparatively speaking, to anyone who can read.

Let us begin by putting aside the various forms of deliberate repression we might lump together under the heading of rhetorical strategy—for example, a writer in a politically oppressed country being forced to speak allegorically, via a subtext, to his countrymen (Anouilh's *Antigone* in Nazi-occupied France); or all forms of verbal irony that express precisely the meaning that has been rhetorically

184

repressed; or the literary character, or author, who arouses emotion by refusing to express it (Cordelia's response to Lear, "Nothing, my lord," or the whole of Swift's *Modest Proposal*). Here I am interested only in unconscious acts of repression or what Laplanche calls "motivated forgetting." To move to an immediate question, is it possible that the act of expressing a feeling (in a dream) or a meaning (in, say, a literary text) may be built on a repressive foundation—or vice versa? Any act of repression involves an act of expression insofar as it produces a sign or an image. But I am concerned here not with the executive act of sign-making or image-making, but with the motivation behind it. On the purely semantic level, the words "express" and "repress" have virtually opposite meanings. My dictionary offers one definition of "express" as "to show by a sign; to symbolize, signify; as the sign + *expresses* addition" and gives one definition of "repress" as "to subdue, to suppress, as to *repress* sedition or rebellion." But might we not say, to make a simple case, that if the sign + expresses addition its signification is founded on an absent − sign (subtraction) that has been suppressed but nevertheless provides the negative ground against which the figure + can only be understood? Or, put another way, the concept of freedom (+) is meaningless without the concept of imprisonment (−), which one must "unconsciously" hold in mind if freedom is to enact the gesture of its release. These are elementary examples of how language continually builds on its own foundations, creating, as Laplanche and Leclaire put it, "the dizzying effect of a dictionary: each word, definition by definition, refers to the others by a series of equivalents,"[1] though here I have emphasized the antonymic reliance of

---

[1] Jean Laplanche and Serge Leclaire, "The Unconscious: A Psychoanalytic Study," *Yale French Studies* 48 (1972): 154.

certain words or concepts on their dialectical opposites.

But to call such a transaction a repression would be an extremely loose use of the term, because what is involved is precisely a cooperation rather than a prevention of meanings. One might even describe it as ironic, in the sense in which Burke says that true irony is based on a "fundamental kinship with the enemy, as one *needs* him, is *indebted* to him, is not merely outside him as an observer but contains him *within,* being consubstantial with him."[2] Opposites, in short, attract, are as essential to the basic operations of thought as resemblances. But to say that they involve repressions would drain the term of all its usefulness as a means of describing a certain act of volitional refusal, whether conscious or unconscious. By this I am not implying that someone might not say "freedom" when he means "imprisonment," or put down a "+" in the checkbook when he is repressing a "−". The issue has nothing to do with the reality of repression as a psychological phenomenon. I am interested here only in where one might draw the line between expressiveness, as an act of approximating meanings and feelings, and repression, as an act of censoring them.

This problem seems to be central if there is to be any understanding outside psychoanalysis of what is meant by this most basic of all its terms. Metaphor and metonymy have become primary working concepts in psychoanalytic criticism, though not so much as tools of analysis as symptoms of repression itself, and the business of textual analysis consists mainly in de-metaphorizing or de-metonymizing the text. Increasingly one reads that metaphor (condensation) and metonymy (displacement) are in them-

[2]Kenneth Burke, *A Grammar of Motives and a Rhetoric of Motives* (Cleveland, Ohio: World, 1962), p. 541.

selves mechanisms of repression or, more conservatively, are *like* mechanisms of repression. But even when likeness is invoked there is little interest in retaining any sense of the difference between an analogy and an identity; repression becomes the motive imputed to all resemblance and to all sliding of signifiers and signifieds into each other, and one has the impression that every metaphor in a text is a "wolf in sheep's clothing"—the metaphor, we may recall, in which Freud clearly *expressed* his conviction that dream images are repressive phenomena.

Or did he? We might take this very metaphor, "wolf in sheep's clothing," as a perfect model of the expressive/repressive problem. It certainly expresses Freud's view that dreams are never innocent or concerned with trivialities, but how does it do this, and what else is contained in the metaphor? One could see it as carrying a repression on at least two different levels. First, on the purely linguistic level, the signification of the sign "wolf"

falls below the bar in the Lacanian algorithm $\frac{S'}{S}$ (if I have it

right) and refers to the threatening nature of the latent content of the sheeplike dream. Thus all metaphors, no matter what their content, are repressions because they leave something unmarked under the bar, something unspoken; all metaphors, we might say, are wolves in sheep's clothing. Second, on the psychic level of the subject (Freud, in this case) there is another possible repression in the carnivorous nature of Freud's "innocent" choice of the wolf metaphor. In choosing a metaphor one not only expresses a resemblance but also (without knowing it, perhaps) chooses a domain (the domain of predation, in this case) that casts a "motivated" halo around the resemblance. It is one thing to say that a dream wears a mask, like an actor, and another to say that it is a wolf in sheep's clothing. And if one could go through Freud and find a host of wolfish metaphors, one might uncover something about Freud that Freud did not know he was saying. On still another level, could we not see the metaphor as tacitly speaking for all psychoanalysis, which is in essence *a search for the wolf in the sheepfold?* Of course, I am carrying the implications to an extreme in order to illustrate the point that the metaphor *could,* like any image, be one of those slits in thought that opens onto the unconscious. In any event, in saying that the wolf metaphor is a model of the problem, as opposed to a proof of the repressive character of metaphor, I mean only that your view will depend on whether you regard all these transactions as connotations of meaning or as repressions of meaning. No one would take issue with the idea that language can be the carrier of signs of absent and unsuspected meaning or thought, in the sense that apparel oft proclaims the man beneath it, whether the man knows it or not, or that one always gives away things about oneself in speaking. But the problem then is to decide when such conscious-unconscious transactions are repressions and when they are simply indications. This is the key point at issue between an expressive and a repressive theory of dreams: is there a free flow of thought from origin to expression, or has there been some form of psychic intervention that alters thought en route to expression? But let us turn to a more complex literary case, one that might go either way, or perhaps even both ways.

In a 1987 issue of *Critical Inquiry* entitled "The Trial(s) of Psychoanalysis," Michael Riffaterre writes about the "intertextual unconscious" in Proust. Strictly speaking, Riffaterre's essay is not psychoanalytic in its orientation. In fact, he is critical of psychoanalytic criticism insofar as it privileges "preconceived categories" (i.e., the Oedipus conflict) that might lead to "an aprioristic reduction of the text to its author, or even of the author to one of the categories delineated by psychoanalytic typology."[3] Still, it comes down to a question not of the unconscious itself but of the analytical method one uses to retrieve it. Riffaterre's thesis is that the analyst would fare better if he or she took the text for what it is and allowed it to speak out of its own organization of signs and affects. His method consists of identifying "anomalies," periphrases, and what he calls syllepses (the co-presence of two meanings for one word) in the text of Proust's novel and treating them as signs of the unconscious:

> In other words, literary signs point to the unconscious inasmuch as they repress a meaning in the process of conveying one. This dual action of the sign is best described as intertextuality: the perception that our reading of a text or textual component (paragraph, sentence, phrase, or word) is complete or satisfactory only if it constrains us to refer to or to cancel out its homologue in the intertext. Recovery of the intertext does not in itself constitute a discovery of the unconscious, but it directs the analyst toward it, and the more such "bearings" are collected along the written line, the easier it is to pinpoint the location of the repressed. Intertextuality, in short, is tantamount to a mimesis of repression (pp. 373–374).

As his central example, Riffaterre offers a fascinating, indeed suspenseful, account of how Proust creates three versions of his mother, all of which are associated with the term "marquise" ("slang for the madame ·of a bawdy house," p. 380) and the illicit sexuality it sylleptically contains. Around these figures swarms "a series of screen images hiding phantasms of oral sexuality" (p. 381). This is hardly the place to do justice to Riffaterre's complex, detailed, and (to me) completely convincing analysis. Nor

---

[3]Michael Riffaterre, "The Intertextual Unconscious," *Critical Inquiry* 13 (Winter 1987): 372.

does the method seem anything less than clear and careful. What I find puzzling, however, is the assumption of repression. I am not sure whether Riffaterre is using the term "repression" in its full psychoanalytic meaning (that is, as the mental process of preventing certain thoughts from reaching awareness) or simply going along with the psychoanalysts and using the term loosely as a metaphor for something he would prefer to call by another name. Is Proust's novel an act of repression, or is it *like* an act of repression? The phrase "tantamount to a mimesis of repression" would indicate the latter, but in that case could we not just as well call it a mimesis of imagination? Are we getting closer to the motive of the novel by likening its tensions (between text and intertext) to a repression?

If we were to go through Riffaterre's text and delete all references to repression and the unconscious, we would find that his reading of Proust remains just as convincing. The vocabulary of psychoanalysis is virtually supererogatory. Once it has been pointed out to you, how can you fail to see the significance, on any interpretive ground, of Marcel giving Aunt Léonie's furniture to the madame of a brothel, one of the pieces being the sofa on which he was "sexually initiated" as an adolescent (p. 380)? But what is the evidence for a repression? I suppose, it is probably Proust himself, and therefore all the heterosex automatically converts to homosex. But might we not assume that *A la recherche du temps perdu* is a novel written by a homosexual about the experience of homosexuality in a substantially heterosexual world, and that Proust was well aware of what he was doing, at least in the way that artists know when the text is "right"? I am sure that Riffaterre would find much of this agreeable because he is aware that the novel is "strongly organized, over-determined by aesthetic, generic, and teleological constraints, and [that] whatever survives of free association is marshaled toward certain effects" (p. 371). But where, then, is the repression? At what point does subtlety of effect—polyphony—become repression? Is the "unsaid, hidden, taboo significance" (p. 381) necessarily repressed? Where exactly is the repression in this succulent passage (quoted by Riffaterre) on Gilberte?

> Recalling, some time later, what I had felt at the time, I identified the impression of having been held for a moment in her mouth, myself, naked . . . , and, when she used my surname . . . her lips . . . seemed to be stripping me, undressing me, like taking the skin off a piece of fruit of which one can swallow only the pulp (p. 382).

One can understand how Marcel, the character, might be unaware of the hidden significance of this memory, of what he was actually doing to Gilberte (or she to him), and one can understand how a reader might experience something like an echo of repression in unconsciously joining all these dimensions of unspoken meaning. Moreover, one can appreciate how the concept of repression may have led Riffaterre to a retrieval of some very delicate materials. My point is that the character of such writing is not necessarily repressive, and that in using the term, even metaphorically, we introduce something surreptitious into what may simply be a sensitive act of imagination. Is this not the very vitality of Proust's art, this "intermittence" of two texts, as Barthes might put it: "the staging of an appearance-as-disapperance"?[4] Imagine a boy in Gilberte's place, and the erotic play of the scene disappears, becomes a scene out of Genet or Bataille.

Regarding vitality, we may also add the vitality of the reader, or of reading itself. Riffaterre is concerned a good

[4]Roland Barthes, *The Pleasure of the Text,* trans. Richard Miller (New York: Hill & Wang, 1975), p. 10.

deal with the reader, and especially the reader who is not trained to look at a text from a psychoanalytic perspective. But somehow one has the sense that it is the text, rather than the reader's response to it, that interests him. One might make the same criticism of Riffaterre's reading of Proust that Jerry Aline Flieger makes of Jean Bellamin-Noel's reading of the dream sequence in *Un Amour de Swann*, that it fails to place the "textual unconscious" in the writing reader. "The reader's enjoyment," Flieger says, "depends on the ability to reproduce the *process* (of writing), to 'work' on the text as the writer has done, in a sort of 'ideational mimetics' of the writing process. The 'textwork' is an active process, and it is shared by a plural writing subject."[5] In Barthesian terms, then, one might say that the so-called textual unconscious is the reader's "ecstasy" in discovering that the text is behaving *as if* it were concealing his or her interpretation.[6]

Maybe there is repression at work in Proust.[7] No one

[5]Jerry Aline Flieger, "Trial and Error: The Case of the Textual Unconscious," *Diacritics,* Spring 1981, p. 64.

[6]The notion of the unconscious being located *in* the reader seems altogether plausible, and much of the argument that follows here could be considered a rhetorical variation of the idea, albeit with strong reservations about the role played by repression in the process of reading. See also Peter Brooks, *Reading for the Plot: Design and Intention in Narrative* (New York: Random House, 1985), esp. pp. 216–237, and Peter Brooks, "The Idea of a Psychoanalytic Criticism," *Critical Inquiry* 13 (Winter 1987): 334–348.

[7]I am taking for granted the repression necessitated by a society in which an author like Proust can speak about his own homosexuality only indirectly, through that of characters like Charlus. There is also the form of repression discussed by Gérard Genette called "projective denial" that enables the character (Legrandin, Charlus, Bloch, etc.) "at one and the same time to expel the guilty passion far from [himself] and to speak of it constantly where others are concerned" (*Figures of Literary Discourse* [New York: Columbia University Press, 1982], p. 279). However, unless the latter can somehow be extended to Proust himself,

can know, even on the level of imaginative intuition, *all* that one is saying, or not saying, and in the gaps there are doubtless traces of an unknown self one would rather not confront. But I do not get a sense of something tantamount to that unknown self from Riffaterre's sexual deconstruction of the novel. In any event, even if I am wrong I would argue that an artist does not necessarily repress when he hides taboos in the thickets of his prose, that if in my ingenuity I can find them they may well have been put there with some degree of deliberateness, the making of art being therapeutic on just the count of its putting everything that matters precisely in its place. Presumably, what most writers want out of every image is as much intertext as possible, and if you are writing thoroughly—ironically—about, say, homosexuality, one of your leading aims would be to create images that express the social (i.e., the prohibitive) as well as the sexual tensions of homosexuality. Homosexuality is not exhausted in its genital activity; it is what one might call a theme of one's being, the world itself being its larger context. And all themes require something *like* repression, that something *not be said,* that something be left out, or under, in order that the text will have an et cetera foundation in the open world—if you will, an extensivity that belongs to the narrative precisely by not appearing in it. The text must be periphrastic and elliptical, not so that it can avoid or repress but so that it can embody otherwise unembodiable connotations.

Let us take a simpler case of a sylleptic text that is not packed with so much biographical or autobiographical significance, a text that might stand for the intertextuality of all texts. For many years editors have been worried about whether Shakespeare intended the word "solid" or "sul-

---

neither of these is a form of unconscious textual repression as I am discussing it here.

lied" in the opening line of Hamlet's first soliloquy. But for almost all interesting artistic purposes, it does not matter, because both words are there whether you want them or not. Probably the least attractive option is "solid" (now out of fashion) because it fits no neatly with "melt" and "thaw." However, "sullied" contains a "solid" by virtue of a phonetic metaphor, and you can see—or rather, hear—how Hamlet might unconsciously arrive at "melt," "thaw," and "resolve"—in other words, how "sullied" could get classified as a solid by the brain (Shakespeare's *and* Hamlet's) and cause Hamlet to embark on more fluid categories through a kind of acoustical pun. Moreover, even if you read the word as "solid" there is more of the same associative confusion, because *"solid,"* in its turn, contains "sullied," "sallied," "sallowed," and probably "soiled," and, sure enough, Hamlet shortly begins talking about sullied things—

> How weary, stale, flat, and unprofitable
> Seem to me all the uses of this world!
> Fie on't, ah, fie; 'tis an unweeded garden
> That grows to seed; things rank and gross in nature
> Possess it merely . . .

—all of which have nothing to do with solidity. My question is, Is this instance of intertextuality "tantamount to a mimesis of repression"? Is it an instance of repression if the mind (character's or author's) cannot "make up its mind" and has it both ways, or, more accurately, if it processes a thought or a sound into two associative categories and insists on pursuing them both? One can even understand how the typesetter might have read "solid" as "sullied," or "sullied" as "solid" (as the case may be) by making a visual error based on one "correct" semantic reading of the text. But I do not see why one should say that such carryings on in the basement of the text, any text, should be charged to an unconscious, unless one is simply using the term "unconscious" as shorthand for the unceasing interplay of sound and sense in the artist's imagination.[8] But perhaps we have not gone far enough. From the standpoint of *sense,* one might find a repression on a still deeper level, the pun on sound simply marking the site of one of the play's key sexual exchanges. For instance, a Lacanian reading (to follow the theme of Lacan's own essay on *Hamlet*) might point out that it is far from accidental that there is confusion between "solid" and "sullied" in Hamlet's mind, especially in the context of "flesh." As Freud said of the asparagus spears, no one needs to be told what "solid" (and/or "sullied") flesh means, and Lacan would surely see the entire soliloquy as prime evidence for his idea that the play is a "mourning for the phallus," specifically the phallus Hamlet has lost.[9] Thus Hamlet is speaking more trenchantly than he knows in confusing the sullied and the solid in relation to melting flesh—not in the hope (to put it one way) that his own erection would go away, but rather his uncle-father's, which has, so to speak, "popp'd" between Hamlet's mother and Hamlet's hopes.

[8]The distinction between the text of Hamlet's soliloquy and its phonemic and connotative subtext seems consistent with Julia Kristeva's semiotic concepts of the *phenotext* and the *genotext.* The phenotext, the phenomenal text itself, "is a structure . . . [that] obeys rules of communication and presupposes a subject of enunciation and an addressee. The genotext, on the other hand, is a process; it moves through zones that have relative and transitory borders and constitutes a *path* that is not restricted to the two poles of univocal information between two full-fledged subjects" (*Revolution in Poetic Language,* trans. Margaret Waller [New York: Columbia University Press, 1984], p. 87). See also Kristeva's discussion of the "semiotic *Chora,*" in ibid., pp. 25–28. What I have already said in Chapter 1 about "inner speech" as an explanation of dream distortion could be considered to belong to the category of the genotext. In fact, what is a dream but a view of the genotext at work?

[9]Jacques Lacan, "Desire and the Interpretation of Desire in *Hamlet,*" *Yale French Studies* 55–56 (1978): 47.

This of course is a Freudian or Jonesian reading. Lacan's own reading is not so conventionally Oedipal. By an adroit chain of analytic moves, Lacan determines that the lost phallus is really "that piece of bait named Ophelia" (p. 11). This is not at all the outrageous claim it may appear to be when isolated from Lacan's own argument. It would take an opaque mind to overlook the fact that Ophelia is persistently associated with phallic imagery and goes to her "muddy death" carrying "dead men's fingers." But the point Lacan develops is that Ophelia is one manifestation of the phallus, it being "everywhere present in the disorder in which we find Hamlet each time he approaches one of the crucial moments of his action" (p. 49). And after reading Lacan, one can certainly see a new respect in which Ophelia "becomes one of the innermost elements in Hamlet's drama, the drama of Hamlet as the man who has lost the way of his desire" (p. 12). In any case, what concerns me here is not Lacan's interpretation but the question of its derivability from the text. As with any provocative reading it is not necessary to endorse it in order to accept it as a *possible* way through the text, especially one as endlessly beckoning as *Hamlet*. But it is quite another thing to say that the text contains the interpretation in a repressed form or, to be more specific (which Lacan does not do), that it is punning on "solid" and "sullied" because the phallus was somehow on Shakespeare's or Hamlet's unconscious mind. There is still the old-fashioned possibility that Hamlet is deeply grieved by his father's death and his mother's remarriage and is thinking about suicide (not necessarily unconnected with sex) and you can follow "solid" and "sullied" down that path as well and see how the confusion makes still another kind of unconscious sense. Then too there is the possibility, again old-fashioned, that Ophelia is, after all, the vagina—that is, she is Woman/Bride/Mother, the woman Hamlet at once loves

("I loved Ophelia . . .") and suspects ("I loved thee
not . . .") as the extension of his mother's frailty. But
neither of these readings cancels the possibility that she
may also be seen as the phallus (Self-as-Other/ Uncle/
Father), which Lacan is suggesting. But this compatibility
of opposites is the condition of any dense text (as one
might make a very convincing case that Hamlet delays and
then argue convincingly that he does not delay at all).[10]
The text is docile, it will allow you to have your way with
it. And if the sign can go both ways, or all ways (within
reason), then what is being repressed beyond the interpretation that one has simply implanted in it? The repressed, in other words, is what was not there until the
critic arrived.

Are we not responding to two-texts-as-one when we
read Lacan (or anyone) on *Hamlet* (or any text)? Thus the
Lacan-Hamlet is a double text held together metaphorically

[10]Lacan would probably find my distinction between Ophelia as vagina and Ophelia as phallus rather frivolous. To Lacan, the phallus, as a
signifier, covers both sexes in complex ways. For example, take the
following passage from Lacan's "Signification of the Phallus": "I am
saying that it is in order to be the phallus, that is to say, the signifier of
the desire of the Other, that a woman will reject an essential part of
femininity, namely, all her attributes in the masquerade. It is for that
which she is not that she wishes to be desired as well as loved. But she
finds the signifier of her own desire in the body of him to whom she
addresses her demand for love" (in *Ecrits: A Selection,* trans. Alan Sheridan [London: Tavistock, 1977], pp. 289–290), or, from the same essay,
"It can be said that [the phallus] is chosen because it is the most tangible
element in the real of [*sic*] sexual copulation, and also the most symbolic
in the literal (typographical) sense of the term, since it is equivalent
there to the (logical) copula. It might also be said that, by virtue of its
turgidity, it is the image of the vital flow as it is transmitted in genera-
tion" (p. 287). This conception has provoked a great deal of comment,
especially among feminist readers. Jane Gallop reviews the controversy
in *Reading Lacan* (Ithaca, N.Y.: Cornell University Press, 1985), esp.
pp. 133–156.

by certain tenors, or points of resemblance between modern phallus psychology (as advanced by Lacan and others) and standard renaissance sexual imagery. These points are neither coincidental nor corroborative in the sense that the renaissance coupling of sex and death, or sexual and floral imagery, confirms modern psychoanalytic theories about phallocentrism, for even without an "unconscious" understanding of these ideas it would surely have occurred to poets to see a metaphorical correspondence between flowers, sex, and death on the basis of a quick glance at Mother Nature. Still *Hamlet* can be read phallocentrically, for there is always a sense in which a "universal" can be applied to a text that may then be said to be a "concrete example" of the universal—or, as I believe psychoanalysis would argue, the universal (here, the "mourning for the phallus") is actually the ur-meaning of the text and the repressed condition of its origin. The problem is that the text is not strictly an example of anything, unless of the categories of text, art, imitation, revenge tragedy, and the like; rather, it is something of a universal in its own right under which a virtually endless series of interpretative "examples" can be placed. The text does not, like the patient in analysis, have a single "nuclear trauma" to be uncovered by "the talking cure." The text does not talk *back*. It has the impassivity of the analyst, and as a consequence a reverse transference occurs in which the interpreter projects into the text his or her own designs. To some extent this is true of all interpretation: the interpreter looks *for* something and finds it by "repressing" everything else, much as the sculptor releases the figure imprisoned in the marble by simply chipping away the excess.[11]

---

[11]Psychoanalytic criticism is well aware of the transferential aspect of reading. As Patrick J. Mahoney notes, "Critics currently differ in their estimate of how much meaning is determined by the text itself and how

Any new reading of a text is thus to some degree a revision of its connotations, the idea being that connotations are continually being extended along a metaphorical vector on which the text serves as tenor for a new vehicle. Some connotations are more or less enduring and transcultural (Hamlet admires Horatio; Claudius is a villain); some are time-bound or culture-bound (Hamlet is a "dreamer," an "absurd man"); and some are simply idiosyncratic (Hamlet and Ophelia have "slept together"; Hamlet is in love with Horatio). But we should not imagine that what we find in a text is *in* it, waiting, in some repressed form. So-called repressed content is only one of an endless series of connections one might make between the unmarked gaps and the articulated markings of a text. The experience of repressed meaning is not even peculiar to "psychological" content and can occur in any reading—political, historical, theological—that uncovers something that had not been seen. The biographical critic will show us how the author has written himself incognito into his text, the New Historical critic may point out the "unconscious" process of self-fashioning, the theological critic will find in the hero's passion an imitation of Christ, and so on. In short, the unconscious of a text is its potential for interpretation, and there are modes of interpretation yet unborn to which the text will one day open itself freely, not because it has contained their findings all along, like ore in the earth, but because interpreters will put their

---

much by the subjective responses of the reader considered either individually or within an interpretive community" (*Freud as a Writer* [Yale University Press, 1987], p. 186). Without claiming to settle this question, I suggest as a rule of thumb that meanings are determined by the text only insofar as it offers a structuration of significant human concerns that is itself the ground from which meaning and interpretation arise.

questions to the text in such a way that it will return obliging answers. By this I do not mean false or forced answers, but conditional answers—answers-in-time, answers dependent on the formulation of "preconceived categories." So Riffaterre, like Derrida before him, is quite right in saying that psychoanalysis finds in a text only what it looks for—itself—but in this it is no different from any other critical persuasion, including Riffaterre's own persuasion that the text is somehow able to stand on its own and that one can look at it with an innocent eye.[12]

I hope it is clear that I am not trying to belittle the achievement of psychoanalytic criticism; nor am I arguing against the concept of repression, which no doubt begins with the individual's first awareness of alterity in the world and rises through sexual and social censorship on all levels of communal life. Moreover, I must add that Lacan does not seem interested in the question of how much Shakespeare may personally have been repressing or how unconsciously he may have understood the principle of phallocentrism. Rather, Lacan is concerned with Hamlet's enigma only as an occasion for working through the problem of "the dialectic of desire" he was pursuing in his seminar. There is even a respect in which the action of desire, as Lacan (or any psychoanalyst) conceives it, could not be detected unless it did not appear in a text, for the basis of desire is that it establishes itself in something other than itself. As Lacan says, the unconscious is the discourse

---

[12]Barbara Johnson's response to Derrida's critique of Lacan and psychoanalysis appears in her "Frame of Reference: Poe, Lacan, Derrida," *Yale French Studies* 55–56 (1978): 457–505. Derrida's claim that psychoanalysis is simply "a repetition of the structure it seeks to analyze" is, Johnson argues, "a profound insight into its very essence. Psychoanalysis is in fact *itself* the primal scene it is seeking: it is the *first* occurrence of what has been repeating itself in the patient without ever having occurred" (pp. 498–499).

of the Other, and desire is the desire of the Other.[13] Imagine a version of *Hamlet* in which Shakespeare or another artist would speak openly about Oedipus, the Mother, castration, and the Phallus—imagine a soliloquy in which Hamlet might say, "I do feel so castrated by this o'erhasty marriage that all the world is like to a phallus"—and the psychoanalytic critic would either lose interest or develop suspicions that something else was going on. In such an assertion we may locate the very lure of the repressed, since the presumption of self-understanding is perhaps the most insecure position one can hold in this world.

As a final illustration of the textual unconscious, let us take a nonliterary case. Suppose I read in a psychoanalytic essay (as one often does) a statement like this: "The unconscious is not a place in the brain that thinks on its own." And suppose the essay goes on to say that, on the contrary, the unconscious, is simply (or complexly) that part of signification that is not articulated or does not appear in the manifest content of a dream, or that the unconscious, as Lacan says, "is neither being, nor non-being, but the unrealized."[14] What is the rhetorical status of this statement—"The unconscious is not a place . . ."? Might there be more here than meets the eye or the ear? That is, if we submit it to psychoanalysis might we not find that it may be unconsciously advancing its own negative? Is it not ambiguously implicating the homuncular meaning of the unconscious in its own declarative discourse of denial (much as a patient might give away Oedipal impulses in the act of denying them), and especially so if the discourse, as it often does, went on to use topographical words like

___

[13]See Lacan, "The Subversion of the Subject and the Dialectic of Desire in the Freudian Unconscious," *Ecrits,* p. 312.

[14]Jacques Lacan, *The Four Fundamental Concepts of Psycho-analysis,* trans. Alan Sheridan (New York: Norton, 1981), p. 30.

"under," "beneath," "in," "down," "descending," and "arising from," all of which point in the direction of a place? Does the significance of such grammatical constructions (here, metaphors for a nonplace) end in their being simply unavoidable, words we must use in order to speak of anything?

At the very least, are we not involved here in what might be called the irony of positive negation? I am thinking particularly of Emile Benveniste's discussion of language in Freudian theory: "The characteristic of linguistic negation is that it can annul only what has been uttered, which it has to set up for the express purpose of suppressing, and that a judgment of nonexistence has necessarily the formal status of a judgment of existence." In short, it is "the fundamental property of language . . . that something corresponds to what is uttered, some thing and not 'nothing.' "[15] Is it possible, then, that simply having in mind this *some thing* that is uttered (and denied) might leave "unconscious" traces in one's thinking about the unconscious, leading one to say one thing, with the clearest of intentions, while thinking *in terms of* another?[16]

I do not intend this to be a roundabout critique of psychoanalytic assumptions (though I realize that my *saying* I

[15]Emile Benveniste, *Problems in General Linguistics,* trans. Mary Elizabeth Meek (Coral Gables, Fl.: University of Miami Press, 1971), p. 73. Freud's own essay on negation, to which Benveniste is here responding, appears in *SE* 19:235–239.

[16]As Daniel Dennett has suggested, you don't get rid of "homuncular" thinking by simply denying the physiological reality of the homunculus. "Driven first from his role as introspector [he reappears] as perceiver, reasoner, intender and knower," even finally in another "concrete form"—for example, "a stimulus-checking mechanism or . . . a brain-writing reader" (D. C. Dennett, *Content and Consciousness* [London: Routledge & Kegan Paul, 1969], p. 99). The homunculus is like a basement or a garage; you clean it out and resolve to keep it clean, but you soon find yourself needing the space for new junk.

don't does not dismiss the possibility that I do). I am simply suggesting what psychoanalysis has insisted on all along, that there is no *manifest* end to signification and that the firmer the statement the more it bears watching. But in this particular case we must surely answer all these questions in the negative: the statement is not a repression, at least in the sense of unconsciously affirming what it consciously denies. The more likely explanation for such statements (if we need one) is that psychoanalysis has historically arrived at the point of cleaning house, ridding itself of theoretical ghosts—however difficult that might be—and that as a consequence there are traces of this exorcistic struggle in its own rhetoric, signaled most clearly in vigorous denials like "The unconscious is not a place" or "The homuncular unconscious is a dead issue." Dead issues, like dead metaphors, live on. So for all reasonable purposes we can grant that the statement is an honest denial and that, as Laplanche and Leclerc would say, it means what it says. Where would we be, after all, if we could not say with some safety that a dog is not a cat or that the unconscious is not a place, or even (on occasion) that a cigar is not a cigar?

I am perhaps misinterpreting what is involved in the principle of repression. What I am trying to understand is the cognitive basis by which we distinguish meanings we can more or less trust and those we are inclined to suspect. If we can agree there *is* a difference—and it is not clear that we can—how does one know where to draw the line? Moreover, beyond that, how can one distinguish an instance of "dynamic" repression, in which the repressed content appears in a censored form, from that passive form of repression that psychoanalysts and linguists have advanced as an elementary principle of all textuality and all speech? Anything "under the bar" belongs to the field of repression: I speak, therefore I repress. But it is not clear how these two forms deserve to be called by the same name. In the former case, repression would constitute a prevention of meanings; in the latter case, it would constitute what I can only assume is an unconscious *ordering* of meanings, because it is simply bizarre to think that all speech is an act of repression in the preventive sense of the word. Should there not be some dimension of speech that is seen to be free of repression if we are to avoid the absurdity of making repression a "universal wolf" (in Ulysses' famous figure) that at last "eats up" the thing it is made of—thought itself? If semiotic repression is simply a metaphor for a text's, or a writer's, act of keeping various connotative significations in play, why not find a term less burdened by all the semantic implications the term "repression" carries with it? What is a repressed signification, in texts like Proust's or Shakespeare's, but a meaning that is fulfilled in the image's metonymic relation to its vicinity? What is the whisper of a "textual unconscious" but the vibration in the reader's mind of a great many resemblances echoing and re-echoing over narrative time and space? Strictly speaking, an act of mimesis cannot itself be a repression. A text in which we discover a repressed meaning cannot have lied to us, and in this it is like the dream. It is one thing to say that on the morning of July 24, 1895, Freud was repressing the real meaning of last night's dream of Irma's injection, but quite another to say that the dream itself was repressing it. It is precisely the dream, in company with the facts behind Freud's published interpretation, that reveals the repression—or reveals his fear of being "franker" about the "further trains of thought" that had occurred to him.[17] But even this is putting it incorrectly. The dream was neither revealing nor repressing the truth; it was simply processing the

[17]Freud, *SE* 4:121.

Fliess-Eckstein affair as a metaphorical structure far wider in its personal implications than the affair itself (serious as it may have been in Freud's immediate life) and therefore something that could only be approximated in composite figures. The dream does not deal in lies or truths, but in what is given as its materials. I may indeed repress, at some level, what my dream has expressed. I may not understand it, or it may perplex me, but it is not censorship that causes my confusion. The dream, like the artist, is simply doing imagination's work. "Don't blame me," the dream might say if it had a voice and were inclined to speak, "I'm just trying to deal with all these competing claims. Go away and let me work."

My complaint about the theory of repression, then, is simply that it is so omnivorous. When I read in a recent psychoanalytic essay that metaphor *is* repression, "the manner of exchange between the conscious and the unconscious,"[18] I wonder whether that is a metaphor or a straight statement and whether the author would agree if we turned it around and said that all repression is a metaphor but all metaphor is not a repression. One might argue, as an overall historical defense, that it is the destiny of all methodologies to appropriate as much of the world as possible. And one can agree that this is how we find things out, by pressing claims to the extreme. But it is similarly our destiny to suspect our claims, and it would seem incumbent on us to put the theory of repression and the unconscious to the most serious question precisely because it is the most unquestioned assumption of our age. Can it be that we have made a metaphor into a reality? It is just possible that the unconscious has become indispensable to

---

[18]Robert Con Davis, "Lacan, Poe, and Narrative Repression," *Contemporary Literary Criticism: Modernism through Poststructuralism* (New York: Longman, 1986), p. 252.

us because so many of our formulations have been built over its abyss, and that it is now a second nature with us, a form of currency through which we are freely encouraged to produce and circulate theories of motivation with as little care about their empirical backing as we have about the gold in Fort Knox.

As for dreaming and art-making, the similarity (or at least the similarity that has occupied me here) ends at the creative stage. And by "creative" I do not mean that loose usage by which we separate "creative" works from other forms of expressiveness, such as criticism or philosophy. Dreaming and art-making are creative processes of imaginative thought, not created products, like the finished poetic image or the philosophical concept. What we have in the poetic image is an artifact of thought whose process is past, but present in the form of a result or a disclosure. The pregnancy of the poetic image rests in the poet's thought (or something like it) resonating again in our own. It is like the mysterious wire of the telephone that is a voice or an ear at either end and a thing in the middle. The dream, on the other hand, exists as a process alone. It cannot be *regarded,* like the poetic image, because it exists only at the point of its formation. In a very real way, in the dream we see ourselves thinking, or we see *what* we are thinking— though this does not occur to us during the dream, and after it we have only a poor memory of an emotion and a scene, which is still another kind of artifact. This is perhaps the reason that we never speak of *making* a dream; instead, by a sort of intuitive redundancy, we say that we *dream a dream,* a wonderful approximation of the dream's way of pulling itself into existence and of the dream's stubborn self-determination. With benign neglect it may pass over my daily sins and gather I know not what trivia of past and present for its own purposes. Once past the notion that the dream is a rebus, the agent of repression, we see how indifferent it is to the core of our immediate needs. Oneiric life, whatever else it offers, is itself an autonomous world; it will consume what memory and invention offer it, and do with it something we do not yet understand. The dream matter-of-factly goes about its business. And like its fellow laborer the heart, which can be metonymically seen as the seat of passion, or of sincerity, or of courage, the dream will cooperatively reduce to anything we like. If you treat it, as the ancients did, as a portent, it will be portentous; if you treat it as a diagnostic symptom, it will yield a diagnosis; if you treat it as a computer, it will compute. All such treatments have a way of becoming cultural synecdoches that innocently take as a whole the part that suits the bias of the moment. And it seems likely that the computer theory too will eventually turn out to be another partial view of the dream born of our enthusiasm for circuitry and information theory in the late twentieth century.

In the meantime, we are faced by as many interesting questions as we have tried to answer. For example, Why should we be invited to certain of our dreams and excluded from others? What exactly is being sorted, updated, and stored via the dream—the images themselves? the dream feeling? the dream structure? none of the above? Although recent advances in neurobiology suggest that dreams are a means of processing experience, we are unable to say why such a process requires visual images or why the brain selects some input for dramatization in a dream and processes other input (things we do not dream but clearly retain) at a nonsensory level. What, indeed, is the function of dramatization? Is it possible that dreams serve purposes similar to those of drama, poetry, and art in waking life? That is, to return to Gadamer's theory of play, is it possible that the dream in some specific way "deepens [the dreamer's] continuity with himself" by putting him in

207

bracketed situations of self-encounter and other-encounter?[19] We tend to think of art as a cultural luxury, something we could conceivably do without—at least more readily than we could do without, say, science. But perhaps a loss of the art-function, if one can imagine such a thing occurring, would eventually produce the same symptoms of distress that occur when the individual is deprived of dream sleep. By art-function I do not simply mean our periodic exposure to works of art, but rather the subtle ways in which we think in the artistic mode or conceive ourselves or the world in imaginative terms—the imitations of children, the daydreams of adults, our perception of the world as being "scenic," "sublime," and so on. Perhaps, as Kundera and Dinesen suggest in my epigraphs, the "unlimited freedom" to imagine "is among mankind's deepest needs." Of course, poets are prone to exaggeration and are therefore not to be trusted in matters of science. But perhaps the proper scientific questions are: Why do we have poets, always and everywhere? What does their activity represent in neurobiological and racial terms? Is it possible that the unlimited freedom to imagine is a requisite of survival in the strict Darwinian sense of that word, and that dreaming and art are its universal manifestations, even in those who do not make art or do not remember that they dream?

While writing this book, I have often been reminded of the scene in Stanley Kubrick's *2001* in which the apeman discovers the principle of the weapon while toying with the bone of a dead animal. In a flash of "primitive" wit, he sees that the bone is a possible improvement over his arm. But under which category of human genius do we place this mental act? Most immediately, it results in the birth of

[19]Hans-Georg Gadamer, *Truth and Method* (New York: Crossroad, 1985), p. 117.

technology, as we see when the apeman euphorically hurls his bone-club into the air following its first successful test in the field. But as it tumbles through the air it is transformed into a bone-white spaceship en route to the moon. We perceive this as a visual metaphor created by the director Kubrick for the purpose of abridging the history of human conquest in the framework of art. But in point of imagination, Kubrick is simply an advanced apeman performing the same act of feature detection that his scientist-ancestor performed one afternoon long ago on the African plain. "All acts of perception," Edelman says, are "acts of creativity," by which he means that it is precisely the brain's "very lack of repetitive precision"—its metaphorical competence, one might say—that allows man to invent his future by re-correlating the perceptual events of his past.[20]

What most intrigues me about the bone-ship image, however, is that it is a spectacular externalization of what must take place in the dreaming brain. Here, literally, we watch the genesis of thought, as clearly as one might watch cell division in a microscope. The difference between the dream image and the film image, however, is that the dream is not such an orderly pursuer of public meanings. Of all mind-states, the dream is the most permissive of the passage of essence from one form to another. Indeed, the dream is remarkable because it has no discretion. If anything, it has a penchant for trivialities, or for confusing trivialities and monstrosities—the habit that psychoanalysis regards as censorship. But this points to a deeper similarity in the possible motives of dream and art: where form is concerned, no image is trivial, no possibility

---

[20]Gerald M. Edelman, "Neural Darwinism: Population Thinking and Higher Brain Function," in *How We Know* (New York: Harper & Row, 1985), p. 24.

too mundane or too monstrous. In the realm of images, the look of the peasant's boot is as compelling an event as the death of Socrates, a perceptual fact that has its analogue in science in Newton's famous affair with the apple. But in art and in the dream this autonomy of the image is made possible by its liberation from the empirical world even as it preserves the laws of that world, or at least the laws of our sensory encounter with it. The basic lesson to be learned from reality is that the trivial and the monstrous have intimate and sudden connections with each other. As the apeman discovered, it is the little things that kill us or assure our survival. Little wonder, then, that the brain should require a mechanism like the dream and that it should be so open-minded about the world, so alert to the possibilities of our facticity.

The conventional symbolism of daylight is that it bathes the world in dependability and clarity. In the day we see exactly what goes with what. But one of the consequences of day-life is that it crowds all being into projects—people, institutions, goals. We are, as the philosophers say, parceled out, distracted by care, and our Being is forfeited to the world. At night, however, we dream and the dream gives rise to an antiworld constructed of figures that are entirely free of the temporal and spatial orders. Let us acknowledge the obvious truth that these figures are made of the "stuff" of the world and that our dreams are made of our worldly cares. We can also say that this is why we make art, but it is self-evident that the experience of art is not exhausted by its referential power. What is of phenomenal interest in the dream is that its figures are set forth with an astonishing intensity of being, at once alien and deeply familiar. In art this is called beauty, but it is achieved in the dream by a virtual reversal of the relation of the eye to the world it scans. Now literally shut and turned inward, the eye is no longer the organ of quotidian sight, but the probe by which consciousness regains its emotional intimacy with the world. One may say that the eye has discovered the power of entering what it has already seen. Reality is no longer what is external to us, and it is no longer circumscribed by the categories of the animate and the inanimate. People are thing-like and things possess consciousness, as in a painting in which the anguish in a face is reflected in the landscape beyond. It is all one to the dream for which anguish is simply a theme, one of the modes of seeing, and the remembered world a field of play in which the brain practices, without thinking about it, the art of thinking.

Index

Index

Dreams (cont.)
and daydreaming, 83; definitions
of, 17, 18n; as diagnostic tool, 30–
34; distortion in, 24–26, 42–47,
passim; emotional vs. intellectual
source of, 115–118; failures in, 50–
53, 139; fake dreams, 31–32; forgetting of, 18, 37, 157–158; fusion
of speech and imagery in, 42–44,
60–62; as guardian of sleep, 16–17,
35, 70; hypnotically induced, 54–
56; as "inner speech," 42–44; irresponsibility of, 136–139; as language, 15–16, 27–30, 34, 42–44,
59–62, 143; learning in, 120–121;
lucid dreams, 39, 135–136; man-
ifest-latent content of, 56–57, 61,
76, 112, 125, 139, 161; meta-experience (world-dreaming) in, 121–
123; no uncanniness in, 45–46;
Parnassian (extratemporal) aspect
of, 47–48, 119, 154; as play
(Gadamer), 126–128, 211; as preservation of experience, 11–12, 17,
25–26, 58, 62–63; problem-solving
in, 115–118, 155; of psychotics,
29, 34–35, 76; as reconstruction of
experience, 25, 109–112, 120–121,
143–145, 171–172, 175; as repres-
sion-free, 20, 177, 204–205, passim; speech in, 42–43; the sublime
in, 78, 113, 122–123; as survival
mechanism, 11–12, 19, 36, 151;
textual validity of, 5, 32–33, 184;
as thought process, 38–40, 50–53,
139, 143–144, 208–211, passim; as
wish-fulfillment, 36, 46, 50, 64,
136n
Dream feelings, 32, 46–48, 107, 111,
113–114, 123, 137, 142, 171–173;
as attitude (Bartlett), 114–115; as
Dionysian knowledge, 181–182;
emotional character of, 115–118,
152; as metaphorical tenor, 141
Dream images, 43, 54; composite
faces in, 146–149; composite
nature of, 44–45, 48–49, 61, 97–
98, 143–145, 167, 176; instability
of, 48–49, 66–68, 97; triviality of,
47; and verbal thought, 60–61, 78;

vividness of, 71, 86, 148–149, 153,
210. See also Dream symbols
Dream plot(s), 49–53, 65–76, 83–84;
as enigma variations, 84, 152–153;
like improvisational acting, 68–69;
irony and, 156–176; metaphoric-
ironic process in, 151; metaphorical nature of, 96–98, 145,
175–176; pedestrian quality of,
152–156; triviality of, 118, 157–
158, 209–210
Dreams discussed: abandoned barn
(author), 112, 140; bathroom (author), 161–166, 172–174; caged
parrot, 53; dancing snakes (Kekule), 115, 117–118; detective
dream (author), 116–117; dying father (author), 136n; Emily's
choker, 103–104, 134, 140; faucet
(Hall), 72–77, 134, 140; flight
(Bachelard), 64, (Merleau-Ponty),
85; French nurse (Freud), 69–70;
garage (Johnson), 157–160; getting
acquainted (author), 109–111;
goose's dream (Freud), 36; Irma's
injection (Freud), 204–205; lady in
Garbo hat, 97–98; lake of truth
(Myers), 134–136, 140; locked revolver (Sartre), 66–67; monster at
large, 67; mother, 48–49; native
spears (Elias Howe), 117; picnic,
55–56; snake in the forest, 46–47,
102; staircase, (Freud), 167–172;
storm at sea (author), 113; unicorn
in forest (Laplanche), 31–32; urina-
tion, 52, 69–70, (author), 161–166
Dream symbols: adaptability of, 31–
32; Freud's concept of, 53–57, 168;
limitations of, 52–53; Sartre's concept of, 65–66; sexual symbols, 48,
54–57, 64, 71–76, 103–104, 138–
139, 161–175, (in Proust) 189–193.
See also Dream images
Dream theories discussed: K. Burke,
51–53; J. P. Changeux, 25–26; C.
Evans, 16–20, 38; S. Freud, see,
Sigmund Freud; C. Hall, 72–73; J.
A. Hobson, 12n; C. Jung, 41; J. F.
Lyotard, 50n; M. Merleau-Ponty,
85; C. M. Myers, 134–135; C.

Index

Kafka, Franz, 20; as dream artist, 45, 77, 135, 180
Kaplan, Bernard, and Heinz Werner, on "inner speech," 42–43, 100–101
Kierkegaard, Søren: on irony, 176–178; on Socratic thought, 38, 60
Klein, D. B., theory of nonimagistic thinking, 20–22, 38, 41
Koestler, Arthur, 175–176
Kristeva, Julia, phenotext and genotext, 195n
Kubrick, Stanley, *2001*, 208–209
Kundera, Milan, 208

Lacan, Jacques, 94, 187; on *Hamlet*, 195–201; on metaphor and metonymy, 132n; on the phallus as signifier, 197n; on the unconscious, 23, 37, 201
Lakoff, George, and Mark Johnson, *Metaphors we Live By*, 8, 107
Language, and dreams, 15–16, 27–30, 34, 42–44, 59–62, 143
Laplanche, Jean, and Serge Leclaire, 31–32, 92, 94, 185; on metonymy, 132n
Latent dream content. *See* Dream(s)
Lyotard, Jean-François, 6, 50n

Magritte, René, as dream artist, 49, 159–160
Mahoney, Patrick J., 198n–199n
Malcolm, Norman, on making judgments in dreams, 136
Manet, Edouard, *Le Déjeuner sur l'herbe*, 56
Manifest dream content. *See* Dream(s)
Mann, Thomas, *Death in Venice*, 178–179
Master tropes: as arithmetic operations, 88–89; combinations of, 130–131; and Freud's dream processes, 6–7; as thought processes, 87–92. *See also* Irony; Metaphor; Metonymy; Synecdoche
Meier, C. A., 115n
Memory, 17, 41, 121; and attitude confirmation, (Bartlett) 118, (Seifert and Schank) 119–120;

Edelman on, 61–62, 95; and imagination, 154; Proustian, 118, 121
Merleau-Ponty, Maurice, on the dream, 85, 121
Metaphor, 87, 88–89, 90, 97, 106, 117–118, 120, 131–149, passim; Kenneth Burke on, 144; as classification mechanism, 128–129; as in condensation, 132n, 186; as displacement, 132; in dreams vs. in poetry, 133–139; as expansion principle, 131–132, 182; and irony, 150–151, 174; and metaphorical deposit, 167–172; as mistake, 139; as privileged trope, 131; in psychoanalysis, 186–188; relation to metonymic process of, 140–143; I. A. Richards on, 133–135; theory-constitutive (in science), 9; Hayden White on, 144
Metonymy, 88–89, 90, 130–131, 145, passim; Kenneth Burke on, 99–100; classical definition of, 99, 155; and Freud's condensation, 100, 186; and Freud's displacement, 132n; Laplanche on, 132n; and metaphorical process, 140–143; and metonymic condensation, 99–105, 106, 112, 150, 158, 164; and Nietzsche's Apollonian principle, 181–182

Nietzsche, Friedrich, on Apollonian-Dionysian, 181–182
Nöel, Bernard, on Magritte, 159
Nonimagistic (nonsensory) thought, 21–22, 37–40, 67, 132, passim
NREM sleep. *See* Sleep

Oedipus complex. *See* Freud, Sigmund
Oedipus story, 174
Ogden, C. K., 98
Ortega y Gasset, José, 129

Palombo, Stanley, 34
Paradoxical sleep. *See* Sleep
Parnassian (extratemporal) principle. *See* Dream(s)
Proust, Marcel: memory in, 118,

121; "metonymic sliding" in (Genette), 142; Riffaterre on, 188–193
Psychoanalysis: Derrida's critique of, 200; and dreams, 3, 9–11, 30–34, 49, 51–52, 165–166; dreams as diagnostic tool in, 30–34; French Freudians, 6, 50, 87n, 93; metaphor and metonymy in, 186–187; pansexualism in, 173; and repression, 184–206; and transference in psychoanalytic criticism, 198–199

Quinn, Arthur, *Figures of Speech*, 88–89

Reiser, Morton F., 10n
Repression: in dreams, 10–12, 20, 24, 34–37, 52, 86, 112–113, 125, 173, passim; dreams free of, 20, 177; expressiveness vs. repression, 184–206; Freud's, 170–171; metaphor as, 93, 186–188, 205; as principle of textuality, 203–204; as "projective denial" (Genette), 192n; "screen memory" as, 125; textual, 184. *See also* Dream(s)
REM sleep. *See* Sleep
Richards, I. A., 98; on metaphor, 133–135; on tropes, 87, 132
Richter, Jean Paul, 77
Ricoeur, Paul: on dreams and language, 30; on feelings, 114–115; on Freudian symbolism, 174–175; on sexual symbolism, 174–175; on the unconscious, 23–24
Riffaterre, Michael, on the intertextual unconscious, 188–193
Rosenfield, Israel, 12n
Rycroft, Charles, on the innocence of dreams, 26–30

Sartre, Jean-Paul, 3; on dream consciousness, 65–67, 153; on hypnagogic imagery, 102; on perception, 86
Schank, Roger C., and Colleen M. Seifert, on knowledge structures, 119–121
Schrötter, K., on hypnotically induced dreams, 55–56
Searle, John R., 22–23

Sexual symbolism. *See* Dream(s)
Shakespeare, William: *Hamlet*, 141–142, 153, 195–199; *Macbeth*, 33, 62, 84; *Measure for Measure*, 91; *Othello*, 163, 178; Sonnet 44, 84; Sonnet 147, 160
Sleep: function of, 17; as liberator, 177; NREM (slow wave) sleep, 152; REM (paradoxical) sleep, 17–19, 42, 59, 85, 121, 151
Sophocles, *Oedipus Rex*, 157
Stekel, Wilhelm, 51–52
Sublime, the, in dreams, 78, 113, 122–123
Swan, Jim, *"Mater* and Nannie," 10n, 169n
Symbols, 63–64, *See also* Dream symbols
Synecdoche, 88–90, 130–131, 145, 150; Kenneth Burke on, 105; and irony, 182–183; part-whole relationship, 107–109, 182; as representation, 104–112; as transformation, 119

Todorov, Tzvetan: on metaphor, 131; on narrative form, 152

Unconscious, the, 188–206; author's critique of, 10–11, 20–57, passim; in hermeneutic definition, 23–24, 36–37; as homunculus, 21–23, 27, 37, 201–203; textual unconscious, 192, 193, 204. *See also* Dream(s); Freud, Sigmund; Lacan, Jacques; Psychoanalysis; Repression

Warnock, Mary, *Imagination*, 88, 154
Werner, Heinz, and Bernard Kaplan, on "inner speech," 42–43, 100–101
White, Hayden, metaphorical conception of history, 144
Winson, Jonathan: on Freud's theory of censorship, 103; on phylogenetic unconscious, 41–42
Wish-fulfillments, dreams as. *See* Dream(s); Freud, Sigmund
Wittgenstein, Ludwig: on Freud's concept of symbolism, 56, 103; on Freud's method, 31